Using Sources Effectively

Strengthening Your Writing and Avoiding Plagiarism

Third Edition

Robert A. Harris

 Pyrczak Publishing

P.O. Box 250430 • Glendale, CA 91225

Although the author and publisher have made every effort to ensure the accuracy and completeness of information contained in this book, we assume no responsibility for errors, inaccuracies, omissions, or any inconsistency herein. Any slights of people, places, or organizations are unintentional. Nothing in this book should be construed as legal advice.

Project Director: Monica Lopez.

Editorial assistance provided by Cheryl Alcorn, Randall R. Bruce, Jenifer Dill, Karen M. Disner, Brenda Koplin, Erica Simmons, and Sharon Young.

Cover design by Robert Kibler and Larry Nichols.

Printed in the United States of America by Malloy, Inc.

ISBN 1-884585-93-0

Contents

Introduction to the Third Edition

Welcome to the third edition of *Using Sources Effectively*. This book is designed to assist you, the writer of a research paper, with practical and effective strategies for incorporating sources into your work. In the chapters that follow, you will learn how the skillful use of sources adds strength to your argument and interest to your writing. You will also learn what you need to know to avoid plagiarism as you bring source material into your research paper. The book includes many examples and ideas to help you make your writing especially good.

Overview of the Book

Chapter 1: The Importance of Using Sources Effectively

This chapter discusses the purposes behind bringing sources into your writing and how the skillful use of quotations, summaries, and paraphrases can give your writing both power and sparkle. By reading this chapter, you should come to view the research process and the use of research materials as an opportunity to enrich your own thinking and provide punch to the arguments you present.

Chapter 2: Finding, Choosing, and Evaluating Sources

This chapter helps you think about the kind of information you need for the paper you will be writing. The purpose of the paper and the intended audience will shape your research. Search strategies both on and beyond the Web are covered, together with a set of guidelines for evaluating the sources you locate.

Chapter 3: Preparing Your Sources

This chapter provides some helpful advice about organizing your research and taking notes in a way that will prevent confusion later. A good note-taking system will make writing the research paper much easier. Also in this chapter is advice about steps you can take to avoid—or defend yourself against—a false charge of plagiarism.

Chapter 4: Quoting Effectively

This chapter covers Why, When, and How to quote a source. Included is a discussion of introductory strategies that will keep your source use fresh. The chapter presents a variety of quoting strategies and ends with the rules for punctuating quotations.

Chapter 5: Paraphrasing and Summarizing

This chapter explores the use of paraphrasing and summarizing as alternatives to quoting. Presented are the Why, When, and How to paraphrase and summarize. Included is information to help you decide when, for a given situation, it is better to quote, paraphrase, or summarize your source. The final section warns writers to avoid the verbal disease of thesaurusitis.

Chapter 6: Avoiding Plagiarism

This chapter provides practical instruction about what does and does not constitute plagiarism. You may be one of the many students who never received formal instruction about plagiarism and how to incorporate sources appropriately. This chapter defines the issues and clarifies some possible misconceptions in order to help you avoid unintentional plagiarism.

Chapter 7: Putting It Together

This chapter shows you how to insert quotations elegantly and effectively into your own writing, following the "simple rule" of marking the boundaries of the quotation to ensure that you are never accused of plagiarism.

Chapter 8: Effective Use

This chapter goes beyond mere compliance with the rules of source use and discusses how to use sources in a powerful and effective way. By employing some of the practical ideas in this chapter, you will be able to write much more vibrant and successful research papers.

Chapter 9: Editing for Accuracy

This chapter offers many tips and reminders about spelling, grammar, and other common errors that tend to slip through unless attention is paid to them. Included are several suggestions for polishing your writing style to make it clear and effective.

New to the Third Edition

New to this edition are the changes made to APA and MLA citation styles since the second edition was released. This edition has also been expanded to include more material on research strategies and source selection (Chapter 2), and more examples of both APA and MLA citation styles. The material on quoting sources has been expanded and is now presented in a separate chapter (Chapter 4). The grammar and mechanics information that was formerly in an appendix has been incorporated into the text as Chapter 9, in part to make the point that editing is an integral component of writing.

Citation and Bibliography Style

The examples in the book are presented in both APA and MLA citation styles, though the book should be a useful resource regardless of the particular style of citation and bibliography you use, whether APA, MLA, CBE, Chicago, Turabian, ASA, or some other. APA style follows the sixth edition of the *Publication Manual of the American Psychological Association* (2010), and MLA style follows the seventh edition of the *MLA Handbook for Writers of Research Papers* (2009). The References page near the end of the book follows APA style.

Acknowledgments

Thanks to Fred Pyrczak, my acquisition editor and publisher, for his continued support for the project and for his helpful comments on the drafts, and to Monica Lopez, project director, for her encouragement and editorial help.

Robert A. Harris
Tustin, California

1

The Importance of
Using Sources Effectively

*The mind is but a barren soil; a soil which is soon exhausted, and
will produce no crop, or only one, unless it be continually fertilized
and enriched with foreign matter.*
    —Sir Joshua Reynolds

The overall goal of this book is to help you write better research papers, principally by incorporating sources into your work more effectively and accurately. However, a preliminary question may have arisen in your mind: Why do you have to write a research paper anyway? Why do instructors assign them? This chapter will provide you with some answers by discussing the benefits of writing a research paper.

- Writing a research paper helps to improve your writing skills.
- Researching brings you new ideas and perspectives.
- Using sources in a paper adds strength, interest, and context to your own ideas.
- Citing sources aids your reader and helps you to avoid plagiarism.
- Writing with sources develops your thinking and analyzing skills.

1.1 Why do research?

Writing—especially research-based writing—is one of the most amazing opportunities you will have in your educational experience. By improving your ability to frame a research problem, locate relevant sources, work with those sources, and write a persuasive paper based on them, you will be developing a host of skills that will serve you well for the rest of your life. Just as swimming is said to be such good exercise because it uses so many different muscles, research-based writing is excellent mental exercise because it develops your skills not just in writing, but in creativity, problem solving, and thinking.

Writing is a thinking process

It has been said that we really do not know what we think about something until we write about it. Writing requires a deeper and more careful thought process than does speaking or even meditating about a topic. By writing down your ideas, you clarify them to yourself or even discover them. More than one student has remarked, "I never knew I thought that," after writing an essay. Writing, then, is an opportunity to strengthen your thinking ability and to extend your mind, to gain a wider view of a subject, to find personal engagement with the world of ideas, even to make the unknown interesting.

When you work with sources, you learn better how to analyze what you are reading, how to evaluate the strength of arguments, and how to fit ideas together with other sources that may disagree. The process of writing a paper based on research materials broadens your understanding of how information is used and makes you more careful about accepting unsupported claims.

Writing is a learning process

Writing is a natural, inseparable part of learning, providing clarity to thinking and solidity to knowing. Writing involves the collection and organization of ideas and thoughts, the analysis of statements and evidence, and the comparing and contrasting of conflicting claims. All of these activities help you learn about a subject. Where before you may have believed that some fact had been clearly established, you discover by researching and writing about it that there are complications to the supposed fact or even more credible alternative explanations of the data behind it.

The act of wide reading, whether in an area of controversy or not, will help you add to your personal database of knowledge and your understanding of the world. When you write a paper that synthesizes your reading, you will learn even more about your topic as you sort out the better arguments from the weaker ones. You will also view the world with more understanding as you gain knowledge. As the proverb says, "The more you know, the better you can see."

Writing develops lifelong skills

The simple truth is this: As an educated person in an ever-more information-driven world, you will be writing for the rest of your life. By developing your writing skills now, you will acquire the competence you need to work effectively in the future. Whatever form your writing eventually takes—whether keyboard, dictation, or a new mind-reading software application—you will need to know how to use all the skills of writing. Thinking, analyzing, organizing, reasoning, using examples—all these and many others are the writing skills that will allow you not just to survive but to flourish.

Writing a research paper also gives you practice in making a subject interesting. In your future writing career, not every topic you are handed will be of interest to you. The subject may not even be immediately interesting to the targeted readers. It is important, then, for you to develop the ability to make a subject interesting both to yourself and to your readers. The more practice you have doing this now, the better you will become at it and the more you will be able to enjoy writing on any topic.

Writing allows you to contribute to the great conversation

Writing represents mental work (creative, analytic, or persuasive) put down in a fixed form so that others can access it at any time and make use of it. Many readers make use of others' writing simply as a means of learning, but many others use writing as building blocks for further knowledge and for their own writing and thinking. This has been true for thousands of years. As the saying goes, "We stand on the shoulders of giants." Nearly every writer makes use of the creative, analytic, or persuasive work of previous writers, building on the thinking and discoveries that have gone before.

Increasingly today, moreover, many writers are building their ideas together. Many corporations are developing knowledge-sharing cultures, where employees can use each other's ideas either by direct collaboration or through the use of knowledge management databases. Developing your writing skills empowers you to become a significant contributor to this creating and sharing of knowledge. The better writer you become, the better writing partner you will be.

Indeed, one of the most common tasks of knowledge workers in the corporate world is to edit source material—policy and procedure documents, checklists, manuals, reports, analyses, and the like—to produce revisions, updates, and extensions. Other documents need to be interpreted and responded to. It is safe to say that you are highly likely to be working with words throughout your career.

1.2 Why use sources in papers?

Understanding the purpose of using sources in papers should result in better papers. Students who believe that sources serve no purpose other than to decorate or lengthen a paper are more likely to insert long quotations without taking much care to build them into the overall presentation. The result of such a practice is, at best, padding and, at worst, a disjointed collage. Sources serve a number of important functions in a paper, both as part of, and in addition to, the requirement that the paper be based on research.

Research sources provide context

Suppose you walk up to two strangers and ask them, "What do you put on your strawberries?" One of them says, "Sugar," and the other says, "Cow manure." How are you to understand this discrepancy? If you think for a moment, you will see that context is crucial to interpretation—a proper understanding of events and thought processes requires knowledge of the surrounding information environment. In this case, one of the strangers puts sugar on the strawberries on the breakfast table, while the other puts cow manure on the strawberries (to fertilize them) in the patch out behind the house.

Similarly, when a scholarly paper describes, analyzes, reports, or argues some point, it does not do so in a vacuum. The topic has almost certainly been treated before, experiments may have been conducted, and other interpretations may have already been made. A first function of the use of sources, then, is to provide background information. An overview, the historical context (which may influence meaning as much as the context of the strawberry comments above), a starting point such as the definition of key concepts—these can all be provided by making use of appropriate sources. In many scholarly projects, a review of the literature is a required first part to provide a history of progress in the field, information relating to the topic, a technical context, or other background for the new material to be presented.

Sources strengthen your argument

One of the myths surrounding research-based writing seems to be that citing sources is a necessary evil, an unfortunate concession required by the rules of composition for giving away credit for ideas. In fact, quite the contrary is true. Using and citing sources actually strengthens your writing in the eyes of your reader, because it demonstrates that you have performed research and have integrated the findings and ideas of others into your own argument.

First, quoting or referring to sources and then discussing them demonstrates that you are aware of other writers' positions on the topic. You are not writing in an intellectual vacuum or off the top of your head, but you have considered the ideas of others in the formulation of your own thinking. Next, using sources demonstrates that your ideas have support. Writers whose ideas parallel your argument add major timber to the intellectual house you are building for your reader. Corroboration of thinking or argument, additional facts or evidence from a third party, and the information of experts all provide powerful support to your position. Finally, using and citing sources demonstrates that you can think and argue along with scholars and other professionals and that you are able to interact with the ideas connected to your subject. Your paper's sources, then, far from being a negative, provide positive evidence for your reader about your researching, writing, and thinking abilities as well as your resourcefulness.

Sources add interest to your paper

As you do your research, you will discover that sources provide much more than factual information or good analysis. Sources often contain stories, personal experiences, unique data, experimental results, tables, graphs, or other items that will add greatly to the interest of your paper. One reason to quote rather than summarize or paraphrase a source is that often the author of the source text has an interesting, colorful, or compelling way of writing. A particular sentence or even a phrase may give just the direct and clear expression of an idea that you need. Even if the source's words are not quotable, you might make the information interesting through an appropriate summary or paraphrase.

Sources provide you with new ideas

As the epigraph at the beginning of this chapter indicates, our minds need the fertilizer of new ideas if we are to be consistently productive in our intellectual lives. Another critical use of sources, then, is that they enrich your mind with new ideas, give you "food for thought," and allow you to compare several different ways of thinking about an issue. Even if all of the research you discover generally agrees with the position you are taking (and that is not likely), you will still be able to refine your own thinking by discovering the various ways of conceptualizing a given idea. More likely, you will encounter ideas and arguments you have never thought of before, providing you with the opportunity to extend your thinking. You may ultimately alter or even reject the original idea you located in your research because sources have suggested a new direction or a new interpretation that is more useful in your argument. (If you should ever develop a love for classical writers such as Plato and Aristotle, you will discover that they are famous not because they are right about everything but because, when they are wrong, they are wrong in very interesting and provocative ways. They make us think.)

Sources reveal controversies

You know the saying, "There are two sides to every argument," meaning that every position has its pros and cons. Even this saying has two sides to it. One side claims that the saying is correct. The other side claims that it is not correct because there are almost never only two sides to a given position: Most areas of controversy have several different sides. A benefit of research and the use of your results is to expose the areas of controversy. By pointing out ideas that conflict with your position and by responding reasonably to those who disagree with your argument, you demonstrate first that you are aware of the opposition and that there is a reasonable response to it, and second that your conclusions are based on a full contemplation of all the evidence, not just on that which agrees with the case you are presenting.

Imagine reading a paper about a controversial issue that completely ignores some strong opposing arguments you have heard elsewhere. What do you think of the paper and its writer? Is the writer simply unaware of the other arguments, and hence has based the paper on partial knowledge? Or is the writer aware of them but has decided not to mention them because there is no adequate response? In blunt terms, is the writer ignorant or dishonest?

See Chapter 8 for information about how to incorporate conflicting sources into your papers.

Sources help you understand how reasoned argument works

The more you work with sources for your research papers, the more information literate you will become. Information literacy is usually defined as the ability to locate, evaluate, and use information appropriately. But the term goes beyond these practices to include an awareness of how information itself works. Specifically, you will discover how a credible argument is assembled, what kind of evidence needs to be brought to bear, how generalizations are formed from experimental samples, and so forth. You will also learn about the role of assumptions, interpretations, and even biases in arguments. (For example, the first time you locate two books each claiming to prove beyond a doubt exactly the opposite conclusion about a controversial subject, you begin to understand much about the world of books and arguments.) Many issues are still unsettled and in flux, and your research will help you become mindful of this.

1.3 Why use sources effectively?

Those who study communication theory will tell you that there is a lot more going on in a research paper or article than the mere conveying of information or mounting of an argument. The way you handle information, how and when you quote, the use you make of a quotation or reference — all these tell your reader not only about your capacity for engaging information, but about your character. If you want to be believed, it is crucial that you write in a way that instills confidence in what you have to say.

Effective use instills trust

Before someone rises to deliver a speech, he or she is almost always introduced. This has been true from the time of the ancient rhetoricians and continues today. The introducer commonly provides the speaker's background, which includes such information as academic credentials, and the source of the speaker's authority or experience relevant to the topic of the speech. In ancient times, this was referred to as providing the speaker's ethos, or character. In other words, the introducer gives reasons why the audience should trust the speaker.

There is a similar practice in publishing, where a book includes a preface or a foreword, often by a notable person, recommending the book to the reader. Moreover, the book jacket includes quotations from reviews favorable to the book. The result is that respected sources help to credential the author — to provide a trustworthy ethos.

When you write a scholarly article or a research paper, you do not have the advantage of another person providing you with a character reference. How you present your material, then, provides the only evidence your reader has about how trustworthy, competent, and fair you are. Not only writing instructors but virtually all careful readers can sense when sources have been carelessly grabbed and dumped into a paper with little thought or analysis. The most authoritative source with the most powerful argument can be substantially diminished by careless or ineffective use. On the other hand, if you are careful, fair, and accurate in the way you use sources, your reader is likely to conclude that you are a reliable interpreter and thinker. When your readers trust you, they are much more likely to accept your argument.

Effective use aids persuasion

The information age is an age of information distrust. We live in an era where misinformation (incorrect, partial, or slanted information) is rampant, and disinformation (information known to be false but presented in order to deceive) seems to be everywhere. Factoids, urban legends, and advertising hyperbole wander constantly through our information universe. So discernment—separating the information sheep from the information goats—is a critical part of the research process. But you need to go further to achieve effective use. If you are to mount a credible claim or believable analysis, you must demonstrate your ability to handle information carefully and accurately. You must show that you possess adequate information-processing skills to interpret, filter, and apply credible sources effectively. In order to take your ideas seriously, your reader must come to believe that you are neither gullible nor sloppy in the way you use information.

Effective use shows your engagement

Using sources effectively—choosing highly relevant quotations, introducing them clearly, and discussing them appropriately—reveals a thoughtful engagement with them after some analysis and judgment. Effective use helps to show that you have performed more than a cursory reading and a perfunctory interaction with the source. Showing that you have taken the time to understand and work with your sources, that you have taken your sources seriously, encourages your reader to take you seriously as well.

Remember that your instructor has spent years reading papers that hastily and sometimes thoughtlessly include quotations and references that seem to be taken out of context or do not quite fit into the student's argument or that seem to be misconstrued. It is all the more important, therefore, to show by your analysis and discussion of each source that you have thought things through.

1.4 Why cite them all?

As you will read again in coming chapters, you must cite the source of each idea or item of information you use, whether you quote, paraphrase, summarize, or merely refer to it. There are several good reasons for this rule.

Cite to help your reader

The primary reason for citing each use of an external source or idea is to provide a path for your reader to follow in the event he or she is interested in further reading. Imagine your reader encountering one of your quotations or a summary of a study and thinking, "That's really interesting. I'd like to read the whole article." Your citation makes exactly that possible. You are providing a courtesy to your reader. Alternatively, instead of interest, you may have inspired indignation in your reader: "How can Jones make that claim?" your reader may demand. Your citation allows your reader to locate the article or book and read the claim in its context.

For most of your academic papers, your instructor will be your immediate, if not your only, reader. Citations perform the same courtesy here. If your instructor becomes interested (or indignant) after reading one of your sources, he or she can go directly to the source for a look. A look at some of your sources will also help your instructor determine how effectively and accurately you are using research material. Your instructor's comments, based on this determination, will help you write better in the future. In these cases, citing sources helps you, too.

Cite to show respect for fellow knowledge workers

At this point in your life, you may not be thinking of yourself as a knowledge worker, either present or future. Yet that is just what you are likely to be. The industrial age has passed, and we now live in an information age where processing information and creating knowledge out of it are major tasks of most educated workers. Just as you would not want others to take and use your ideas or writing without crediting you, you should not take the ideas or writing of others without crediting them. It is a matter of respect.

As mentioned earlier, more and more knowledge is being created through collaboration with others. A key to the willingness of others to collaborate is the feeling that their intellectual property (their words and ideas) will be duly respected and credited. In a corporate environment, where creativity and originality are highly valued, both you and your collaborators will want to work on joint writing projects where each contributor can trust the others to give credit willingly and clearly to the others' ideas. In circumstances where coworkers believe their ideas will be stolen, they will be unlikely to share them.

Cite to avoid plagiarism

A fundamental requirement of academic work is that you clearly distinguish your words and ideas from those of the sources you use. Citation provides the basic mechanism of distinction. A substantial amount of plagiarism is committed unintentionally, simply because the writer did not know the rules or forms of citation. Yet the penalty for such behavior is often severe because plagiarism is considered one of the most serious forms of academic dishonesty. Therefore, out of self-interest and self-protection, you want to be sure to cite your sources. (Plagiarism and the requirements for citation to avoid it are discussed in detail in Chapter 6.)

1.5 Are sources the whole idea?

At least a few students approach research paper assignments with the belief that their own ideas do not count: They think a research paper is to be filled with sources elegantly—and sometimes not so elegantly—strung together. These students seem to fear they will be graded down if even one of their own thoughts gets in the way of the sources. This idea is wrong, incorrect, and not true.

Your thinking is the star

You will recall from above that sources were said to support your thinking. Think of your research paper as a major motion picture. Your thinking, perhaps your central idea, is the star, while the sources you use are the supporting cast. The most important part of a research paper is not the sources themselves but what you do with them. You should use sources to support your own line of argument, your own conclusions, your own ideas. This is your paper we are talking about, not an extended summary of other papers. You are not writing *Bartlett's Familiar Quotations*: That has already been done.

Another way of thinking about your use of sources is to say that just as you should honor the thinking of others by citing their ideas, so you should also honor your own thinking by presenting it clearly and supporting it with research. The sources you cite give solidity, credibility, and nuance to your presentation, but at the end of the day, even though we like your friends, we've come to hear *you* talk.

Sources need something to support

To accept that your ideas are the star in a research paper is to throw down a gauntlet of challenge to yourself: You must produce the star—the ideas. That is, as you research and write, you must supply not only the central idea you wish to advance, but also the analysis, synthesis, fresh insights, interpretations, conclusions, reasons, examples, and other information that drive your central idea forward and that are supported by your research. When you bring in a source, it should have a clear role in adding weight and credibility to your line of thinking or argument.

Sources need interpreting

Henry Ford is credited with having said, "Thinking is the hardest work there is, which is why so few people do it." If he is correct, that may explain why so many research papers handed in to instructors contain little more than a series of thoughtlessly pasted-together quotations. Do not let your papers descend to this level. Take the time to explain the source, to show how it fits into your discussion, and why it was important to bring it into your paper. Otherwise, you will lose most of the benefits of writing a research paper while reducing your workload only slightly.

When you think of yourself in the role of the writer of a research paper, do not picture yourself as an antiquarian collector of old quotations fit to be put on display, but as a detective, a solver of a puzzle, making sense out of many different elements of information. So much information, so many viewpoints, all this raw data in need of explanation—all the materials you locate in your research need more than just organizing; they also require sorting out and applying to a central conclusion. Much thinking and much writing must come in connection with the use of your sources as you explain the meaning, implications, and effect of each one. Forget the staplers (those who would merely staple together an assortment of source materials); you are the weaver of a beautiful and sensible tapestry. You must ultimately tell the story that the sources have helped you to discover.

Review questions

To see how well you understand this chapter, attempt to answer each of the following questions without referring to the text. (Write down your answers to make checking easier.) Then check your answers with the text. If you missed something important, add it to your answer.

1. What advantages are provided by learning how to write well?

2. What are the benefits sources provide to a researcher?

3. Explain how the use of sources strengthens your writing.

4. Discuss the reasons for citing sources.

5. What is meant by the statement, "Your thinking is the star"?

Questions for thought and discussion

Use these questions for in-class or small-group discussion, or for stimulating your own thinking.

1. Think about the last paper you wrote. Apart from the new knowledge you gained about the subject, did you gain anything else, such as improved thinking skills or stronger writing skills?

2. Have you ever written a research paper where you commented very little on your sources? If so, do you think you learned less than if you had written more about the sources?

3. Has this chapter made you more enthusiastic about writing a research paper? Why or why not?

4. Has this chapter convinced you of the value of citation? Why or why not?

Name _____   Course _____

Chapter 1 Review: True-false quiz

Directions: In each case, determine whether each statement below is true or false.

1. Citations are merely for academic accountability and do not help the reader of the paper.
   ☐ True   ☐ False

2. All the sources used in a research paper should support the writer's ideas.
   ☐ True   ☐ False

3. Citing sources weakens the writer's own argument.
   ☐ True   ☐ False

4. A writer's own ideas are stimulated by reading others' ideas.
   ☐ True   ☐ False

5. Citing the sources used in a paper is important for avoiding plagiarism.
   ☐ True   ☐ False

6. Mentioning opposing sources in a paper on a controversial topic weakens the paper.
   ☐ True   ☐ False

7. Knowing how to write well is an academic skill that usually will have little application after graduation.
   ☐ True   ☐ False

8. Writing helps people discover what they think about a subject.
   ☐ True   ☐ False

9. Because a research paper relies heavily on sources, it will therefore have little or nothing original in it.
   ☐ True   ☐ False

10. Because most of your sources are written by highly educated writers, you will not need to explain what a quotation means.
    ☐ True   ☐ False

Self-Assessments

On the following pages are several self-assessments you can take to determine your attitudes and knowledge about plagiarism and citation requirements. After you have read this book and worked through the exercises, you can take these assessments again to measure what you have learned. A preliminary assessment is valuable for learning about what you already know and what you still need to know. It also focuses your attention on the important concepts, so that as you read this book you will be on the alert. A postassessment is valuable for discovering what you have learned. You can compare your pre- and postscores to learn how your attitudes and knowledge have changed.

Name _____   Course _____

Self-Assessment: Researched writing survey

Directions: This survey is designed to discover how confident you now feel about several skills and tasks related to the writing process. There are no right or wrong answers. Please respond to each question by putting a mark at a point along the scale that best represents your opinion.

1. When you are assigned a research paper in a course, do you welcome it as an opportunity to learn, or do you see it as a burden or unwelcome task?

   Welcome   Neutral   Unwelcome
   □ ------------ □ ------------□ ------------ □ ------------ □ ------------ □ ------------ □

2. How confident are you in your ability to use supporting material (quotations, examples, research) effectively to strengthen your ideas in a paper?

   Very Confident   Neutral   Not At All Confident
   □ ------------ □ ------------□ ------------ □ ------------ □ ------------ □ ------------ □

3. How confident are you in your ability to paraphrase an idea for use in a research paper?

   Very Confident   Neutral   Not At All Confident
   □ ------------ □ ------------□ ------------ □ ------------ □ ------------ □ ------------ □

4. How much formal training have you had regarding plagiarism and how to avoid it?

   Much   Some   None
   □ ------------ □ ------------□ ------------ □ ------------ □ ------------ □ ------------ □

5. In writing a research paper, how easy have you found it to incorporate sources that conflict with your central argument or idea?

   Very Easy   Somewhat Challenging   Very Difficult
   □ ------------ □ ------------□ ------------ □ ------------ □ ------------ □ ------------ □

6. How confident are you that you know the rules for using sources well enough to avoid unintentional plagiarism?

   Very Confident   Neutral   Not At All Confident
   □ ------------ □ ------------□ ------------ □ ------------ □ ------------ □ ------------ □

Name _____   Course _____

Self-Assessment: Rules of citation quiz

Directions: Based on your knowledge, decide whether each statement is true or false.

1. When you use an idea you found in a source, you do **not** need to cite the idea if you put it entirely into your own words.
   ☐ True   ☐ False

2. As long as you put the author's name at the end of the paragraph, you may use the author's exact words, without needing quotation marks or a block indentation.
   ☐ True   ☐ False

3. In a research paper, you must cite every fact and idea that is not your own, such as the date Pearl Harbor was attacked by the Japanese.
   ☐ True   ☐ False

4. If you copy a paragraph from an old work that is no longer copyrighted, you still must show it as quoted and cite it, even though it is now in the public domain.
   ☐ True   ☐ False

5. Anything posted on the Web is common knowledge and therefore can be used without citation.
   ☐ True   ☐ False

6. Common knowledge does not need to be cited, unless you quote the exact words of the source (such as an encyclopedia).
   ☐ True   ☐ False

7. If a source presents your own opinion better than you could express it, then you can copy those words into your paper without quotation marks or citation.
   ☐ True   ☐ False

8. If you summarize the general argument of a book into a paragraph of your own words, you still must cite the source.
   ☐ True   ☐ False

9. Plagiarism refers only to copying a source's words without citation: You cannot plagiarize ideas.
   ☐ True   ☐ False

10. There is no such thing as "unintentional plagiarism."
    ☐ True   ☐ False

11. If you copy a drawing or map and use it in your paper, you must cite the source because those are also forms of ideas.
    ☐ True   ☐ False

Name _____   Course _____

Self-Assessment: Plagiarism attitude scale

Directions: This is a measure of your opinions and attitudes about plagiarism. It is not a test. There are no right or wrong answers. Please indicate your honest opinion about each item.

1. I might accidentally commit plagiarism because I'm **not** sure what it is.
   ☐ Strongly Agree   ☐ Agree   ☐ Neutral   ☐ Disagree   ☐ Strongly Disagree

2. Cheating on a test is a worse offense than copying a few paragraphs from a source into one's paper without citing them.
   ☐ Strongly Agree   ☐ Agree   ☐ Neutral   ☐ Disagree   ☐ Strongly Disagree

3. I would never knowingly commit plagiarism.
   ☐ Strongly Agree   ☐ Agree   ☐ Neutral   ☐ Disagree   ☐ Strongly Disagree

4. Plagiarism is important only to people trying to protect their profits through copyright laws.
   ☐ Strongly Agree   ☐ Agree   ☐ Neutral   ☐ Disagree   ☐ Strongly Disagree

5. If plagiarism were widespread at a school, a student would be justified in plagiarizing in order to keep up with the competition.
   ☐ Strongly Agree   ☐ Agree   ☐ Neutral   ☐ Disagree   ☐ Strongly Disagree

6. If my roommate gives me permission to use his or her paper for one of my classes, I don't think there is anything wrong with doing that.
   ☐ Strongly Agree   ☐ Agree   ☐ Neutral   ☐ Disagree   ☐ Strongly Disagree

7. Plagiarism is against my ethical values.
   ☐ Strongly Agree   ☐ Agree   ☐ Neutral   ☐ Disagree   ☐ Strongly Disagree

8. It's okay to use something you have written in the past to fulfill a new assignment because you can't plagiarize yourself.
   ☐ Strongly Agree   ☐ Agree   ☐ Neutral   ☐ Disagree   ☐ Strongly Disagree

9. If I lend a paper to another student to look at, and then that student turns it in as his or her own and is caught, I should **not** be punished also.
   ☐ Strongly Agree   ☐ Agree   ☐ Neutral   ☐ Disagree   ☐ Strongly Disagree

10. Even if they never get caught, plagiarizers cheat themselves.
    ☐ Strongly Agree   ☐ Agree   ☐ Neutral   ☐ Disagree   ☐ Strongly Disagree

11. Students caught plagiarizing should be punished as harshly as other cheaters.
    ☐ Strongly Agree   ☐ Agree   ☐ Neutral   ☐ Disagree   ☐ Strongly Disagree

2
Finding, Choosing,
and Evaluating Sources

There is no less invention in aptly applying a thought found in a book, than in being the first author of the thought.
—Pierre Bayle

Both the enormous quantity of information now available and its wide range of quality make the task of choosing sources wisely more important than ever. This chapter offers some guidelines and ideas for helping to choose useful and high-quality sources.

- ◆ Thinking about the purpose and audience of your paper will help guide your research.
- ◆ Choosing appropriate types of sources will give you better materials to use in your papers.
- ◆ Using a good search strategy will provide you with the sources you need.
- ◆ Evaluating the quality and credibility of the sources is important.

2.1 Start with the end in mind

Before you grab a topic and rush off to the library or computer to look up something about it, think about the kind of product you want to create. Read your paper assignment carefully, and if necessary, discuss it with your instructor. The following considerations will help you in your thought process and in your research and writing.

What is the purpose of the paper?

Why, exactly, are you writing this paper (other than the fact that it has been assigned)? Think about some of these questions:

- ◆ Are you going to write a review, a summary, an analysis, a persuasive argument? A review or summary will be more focused on responding to the work of others, while an analysis or persuasive argument will contain more of your own ideas. A review or summary will engage a limited number of works (or even one), often chosen for their important content as a whole. An argument might make use of ideas drawn from many works.
- ◆ Is the paper going to focus on reasoned argument or factual evidence (or both)? That is, should the discussion be more philosophical, drawing on logic and reasoning more than research, or will it need substantial amounts of supporting data from research and experimentation?
- ◆ Will you do a broad survey or engage in an intense examination of a small detail? For example, are you going to examine the changing views toward authority over time in a nation state, or will you be explicating a sonnet?

How you answer these questions will determine which sources you look for. Your instructor will probably help you with these questions by providing some assignment guidelines, but you might want to clarify your purpose further to avoid unnecessary searching. Ask yourself, "Just what is it that I want to do in this paper, and what kinds of sources will help me?" and write out a few notes that will help guide your research.

What are the expectations of your audience?

The question, "Who is my audience and what does my audience expect?" is one of the most crucial and most often neglected questions any writer faces. Don't be tempted to dismiss the question because it seems obvious that your instructor is the audience. There are several potential audiences for an academic research paper:

- your instructor, of course
- your peers (fellow classmates)
- your friends and dormmates
- a general audience, perhaps
- other professionals in the subject area

With regard to this last possibility, when you write upper division or graduate papers at a college or university, it is usually understood that you are preparing yourself for the great conversation—communicating with the other professionals and experts in your chosen field. So they are, at least in theory, part of your audience. This audience will expect excellence—careful thinking, thorough research, and apt use of that research.

If your assignment involves writing for a general audience, consider issues like these:

- Will you need to include some general information about the topic to provide background or context?
- Will your audience understand the technical jargon that accompanies the subject?
- How will a general audience's preconceptions, knowledge, and lack of knowledge affect the sequence and approach you will need to take in order to be clear and convincing?

Briefly, then, first think about what you want the final product to look like before you take the first steps in creating it. A powerful idea in problem-solving theory is to imagine that you have already solved the problem and then ask yourself what happened that enabled the solution to occur. Similarly, you might imagine having already written an excellent paper—that perhaps has won a class or campus-wide award, or even been accepted for publication—and then ask yourself how you worked on it and what you put into it that helped bring about such success.

2.2 Select the kinds of sources you need

The saying, "All sources look alike on a computer screen," cautions us to be careful to consider the wide range of materials available—both in kind and in quality—and to select those that best suit the task at hand. Resist the temptation to use just any sources that you locate; take some time to think about the kinds of information you need and how well the sources you locate meet those needs.

Choose the kind of information you need

For building a solid research paper, you will need facts, of course, but you will also want expert interpretation of some of those facts, together with professional judgments about the importance of the information you are discussing. You may want reasoned arguments, creative ideas, personal examples, accounts of events, experiments, philosophical commentary, and so forth. Many sources contain more than one of these kinds of information, while others focus largely on one or two. If you keep in mind what kind of information you are seeking, you will be able to select sources more quickly and more effectively from among the items you locate.

Choose appropriate primary and secondary sources

A primary source is an original source of information. Examples of primary sources include a historical document, an account of a laboratory experiment, a literary work, an eyewitness account, the original proposal of a new idea, or other original work. A great example is the more than one million photographs and prints available online at the Library of Congress Digital Collection (www.loc.gov). Another primary source is the federal government's statistical database Fedstats (www.fedstats.gov), containing statistics from more than 100 federal agencies.

A secondary source offers a summary of several primary sources, or an interpretation of or commentary on one or more primary sources. Examples of secondary sources include encyclopedia articles that rely on a number of primary sources to construct a historical narrative, a work of literary criticism, and works that popularize newly reported discoveries or newly presented ideas.

Depending on the subject, the class level, the instructor, and a number of other factors, you may be using more of one kind of source than the other. Many instructors view the research paper as the construction of a secondary source, analyzing and commenting on a set of primary sources. In a literature course, you might use secondary sources to support your interpretation of a literary work (the primary source) as you create a secondary source of your own. In a history course, you might use both primary sources (laws, letters, diaries, works written during the period under study) and secondary sources (interpretive works by modern historians) to construct a paper. In the social and behavioral sciences, you might use primary sources (reports of empirical or original studies) and create some primary source material yourself by conducting your own experiment, observation, or interview.

When you have a choice, the use of primary sources is usually superior because you are dealing directly with the original work or evidence rather than seeing it through the lens of another interpreter. For this reason, relying on general encyclopedias for sources is often frowned upon because the articles in them are secondary sources or are themselves based on secondary sources. (Using an encyclopedia to get an overview, background information, ideas for the direction you want to take, or the consensus of current thought, is an excellent idea. However, your research should then go far beyond that.)

One caution is in order, however. The mere fact that a source is primary or original rather than secondary does not automatically grant it immunity from evaluation. Eyewitness accounts might be biased, original experiments might be flawed, a historical photograph might be misleading (even though it has not been Photoshopped). Just as an eye opener, you might search a newspaper database or the general Web using the exact phrase "study was flawed" and examine the results.

Choose sources of appropriate scholarship

Whether printed or online, publications exist along a range or at various levels of scholarliness. The concept of scholarliness refers to the level of expertise, learning, and evidence brought to bear on a subject as well as the intended audience and even the nature of the information itself. After all, the purpose of some information is to entertain—to tell a good story—rather than to get the facts right. Generally speaking, the more scholarly a work, the more care is taken with accuracy and completeness.

The chart below will give you an idea of the range of informational materials and how their audiences and purposes vary.

VARIETY OF SCHOLARLINESS IN SOURCES

Professional	Substantive	Popular	Sensational
Written by academics, scientists, or experts	Written by staff writer or expert	Written by staff writer or freelance journalist	Written by staff writer or freelance writer
Audience is other academics or those trained in the field	Audience is the well-educated public	Audience is general reader	Audience is less well educated
Purpose is to share findings or present theories: to inform	Purpose is to inform and entertain	Purpose is to entertain and inform	Purpose is to entertain
Discussion is often highly specific and sophisticated	Discussion is more general, easier to understand	Discussion is general and simplified	Discussion is sensational and simplistic
Bibliography of sources is always included	Some sources are cited	Sources are often not cited	Sources are not cited
Article has been peer-reviewed or refereed by other scholars in the field	Article has been approved by an editorial board	Article has been approved by an editorial board or editor	Article has been approved by an editor

You should not take this chart too literally: There are not exactly four kinds of publications, and there are exceptions to most of the comments made here. However, the chart can serve as a general model to give you a good sense of how the source, purpose, and quality of information vary. For much of your research, it is a good idea to restrict yourself to sources of a professional or substantive variety. Occasionally, popular magazines offer useful material; but as entertainment values take on more importance than informational values, the degree of reliability of a source can suffer.

ASK A LIBRARIAN

An excellent way to get help in locating and selecting good sources is to talk with a reference librarian. Librarians have expertise in searching for and evaluating information, and they are also familiar with the library's collection of materials, the subject guides, online databases, and more. A suggestion such as, "You might check Special Collections for that," or "If you can't find that Web page anymore, check the Wayback Machine at the Internet Archive," can be a priceless timesaver and resource. And there's no better way to get pointed in the right direction than to discuss your research with someone who knows information sources inside and out. A chat with a reference librarian will also help you narrow down an overly broad or unfocused topic.

Avoid choosing a source simply because you agree with it

If the sources you use are to add strength to your writing, they must be robustly credible, well reasoned, and fair. You may find sources that support the direction of your argument but that are unworthy of use because they lack the qualities that will gain your reader's confidence. When you refer to a source, you are saying something about the source (that it is worth listening to) and about yourself (that your judgment has approved its use in a formal presentation). In other words, a little of each source you use rubs off on you and your authorial reputation. If you use good sources, your reader will think better of you, seeing you as smart, educated, and discerning.

Avoid quoting standard dictionaries

Would you like to know the easiest way to make almost any instructor or educated reader cringe? Simply begin your paper with, "According to Webster's dictionary, the word _____ means. . . ." Why is this? Consider the reasons for not quoting a dictionary:

- **Readers have their own dictionaries.** It is assumed that readers have a desk dictionary handy, or that they can quickly go to any of several online dictionaries (such as www.dictionary.com or www.merriam-webster.com) and that if all that is wanted is a standard dictionary definition, they can look up the word themselves.

- **Most dictionary definitions are unhelpful.** Many definitions are, in fact, circular. "Wonderful: exciting wonder"; "Heartbreaker: a person causing heartbreak"; "Heater: an apparatus for heating." Even definitions that are not circular like these are often so condensed, generalized, or vague that they do not come near the meaning of the word as you are planning to develop it.

- **Dictionary definitions are descriptive and not prescriptive.** This means that if enough people use a word in a certain way, the dictionary will eventually list it, even though the word has not meant that in the past. For example, some dictionaries now list *imply* as one of the acceptable meanings of *infer*, and some list *continual* and *continuous* as having the same meaning.

- **You can write a better definition.** If you need the definition of an ordinary word, your own definition will be better. For everyday terms, such as *love, justice,* or *philanthropy,* a little thought and effort will produce a much better definition than that found in a typical desk or online dictionary.

- **Scholarly definitions are superior.** If you need a more specialized definition, consult a specialty dictionary, such as the *APA Dictionary of Psychology* (VandenBos, 2007). There are specialized works like this in many fields. You might also quote the definition of a key term from a scholarly article. Scholarly definitions are often extensive and focused, and therefore quite helpful.

♦ **Quoting a dictionary is a red flag.** Quoting a definition at the beginning of a paper implies to an educated reader that the writer does not know how to start a paper (or continue a thought) and is falling back on what amounts to a cliché, and a thoughtless one at that. A paper (or speech, for that matter) beginning with "According to Webster's dictionary" tells the reader (or hearer) that the writer did not put much thought or research into the product and that there is little to be hoped for in the rest of the writer's performance.

♦ **Noah Webster died in 1843.** The name *Webster's Dictionary* is in the public domain and can be used by any publisher for any dictionary. It is now a generic brand and conveys no specific authority.

From these reasons, you can see that quoting a dictionary will actually weaken your writing, not strengthen it.

2.3 Search strategies

When starting a research project, there is sometimes a temptation to sit down at a computer, bring up your favorite search tool, and type in the first word or phrase that occurs to you. Let's take a few minutes to look at a better way of finding relevant and high-quality sources.

Consider the variety of sources

The first task before you begin any research on your topic is to consider what a source is, where sources may be located, and which sources are likely to provide you with the answers or information you want. Let's ask each of these questions in turn.

First, what is an information source? A source can indeed be a Web page you found by googling your search topic, but there are many other kinds of sources. As the table below indicates, not all sources are available electronically. Some are physical, such as books on a library shelf, and others are even alive and human, as in a lecturer or interviewee. A source can be any person, place, or thing that supplies you with information.

SOURCES OF INFORMATION

Audio recording	Newspaper
Blog	Online book or ebook
Dataset	Online journal
Data table	Photograph
Drawing	Podcast
Experiment	Printed book
Film	Printed journal
Graph	Speech or lecture
Interview	Video
Magazine	Web site or Web article

Next, where are sources located? The temptation these days is to "find it online," and ignore any source that cannot be found through a computer search. But as the table above indicates, sources can be found far and wide. Depending on the nature of your topic, you might want to make use of library card catalogs, library stacks, bookstores, museums, art galleries, lectures, phone interviews, or photographic or video archives.

Which sources are likely to provide you with the answers or information you want? Before you begin your research, take at least a few minutes to write a description of the kind of information you're looking for. Then ask yourself, where is this information likely to be found? Some sources, such as refereed journal articles, will provide expert information and the analysis of experiments. Other sources, such as Weblogs (blogs), will provide raw data for analysis and commentary. Even old and out-of-date books can be useful if you are looking for information about the spirit of the age or a particular era's concerns and attitudes.

Now that you're ready to go forth and find the sources you need, consider this hard-won rule from the research trenches:

Rule #1: Keep track of your searches

You have probably heard that irritating saying, "There's never time to do it right the first time, but there's always time to do it over." In order to avoid quoting this to yourself because you have to repeat a search you didn't record, keep careful track of the searches you perform, together with the results. Setting up a tracking log in a spreadsheet or even a word processing document will make organizing things very easy. Here is an example of a tracking log with a few sample entries:

PROJECT: Metacognition and Learning: Activities That Increase Retention				
Date	Database	Search String	Results	Notes
9/26	EBSCO Host: MasterFile Premier & Acad Search Elite	metacognition AND activities	41 hits. Reviewed all.	Saved pdf of Wall and Higgins (2006): Wall-Higgins.pdf
9/26	EBSCO Host: MasterFile Premier & Acad Search Elite	metacognitive AND tools	27 hits. Reviewed all.	Saved pdf of White and Frederiksen (2005): WhiteFred.pdf
9/26	BUBL: Categories 153, 370.7 and 374	metacognition AND activities	Category 374 returned broken link	Many databases. Look again with alternate strings.

Looking online

The computer has certainly made researching easier with the availability of many online databases containing articles from peer-reviewed or refereed journals, not to mention the enormous amount of information available on the general World Wide Web. However, an important caution about searching online must be raised. When you click on a link in the search results and a Web site or document appears on your screen, you must take a moment to evaluate what you're looking at. An article filled with half-truths, misunderstandings, and exaggerations can look the same as—or even better than—an article from a well-respected encyclopedia or scholarly journal. A sophisticated-looking Web site can create the *simulation of authority* when in fact it has little or none. That old proverb about not judging a book by its cover has new use in its updated form: Don't judge an information source by its design.

Phrase the search terms effectively

Whenever you use an electronic database—library card catalog, professional database such as ProQuest, or a search tool for the Web itself—how you phrase your search will have a dramatic effect on the results you get. Follow the advice here to create the best possible search strings:

♦ **Know how the search tool works.** Most search tools have a Help page that describes how to perform a simple search and an advanced search. For example, if you enter the two-word phrase *unemployment insurance*, does the search tool parse this as *unemployment OR insurance, unemployment AND insurance* or the exact phrase *"unemployment insurance"*? For online databases, is the search tool applying your search terms to the title, the author, the abstract, or the full text of the article? Is it selectable? Taking a little time to read the search tool's Help page is always worthwhile.

♦ **Find out which Boolean operators the tool uses.** For advanced searches, you will want to create search strings of somewhat more sophistication than a single word or phrase. Search phrases are constructed by combining search terms with Boolean operators. The table below shows the most common of these operators and the effect they have on a search result. Note that a given search tool might use other operators. Google, for example, parses the plus sign (+) before a word to mean that the word must be included somewhere on the page in order for the result to be generated. Thus, the search expression *+Aztec calendar* would tell Google to return pages that must contain the word *Aztec* with a preference for pages with the word *calendar*, also.

BOOLEAN OPERATORS

Operator	Example	Returns results with
AND	depression **AND** dopamine	both terms, none with only one of the terms
OR	Splenda **OR** sucralose	either term or both terms
NOT	Washington **NOT** George	Washington except those with George
NEAR	flu **NEAR** vaccine	terms within a set number of words of each other
ADJ	word **ADJ** root	terms adjacent (next to each other) in either order

---

Boolean Tip: As the table above shows, the AND operator *restricts or narrows* the search, while the OR operator *expands or widens* the search. Be careful not to get these backwards.

♦ **Remember to include the word variants.** The exact word form or phrase might not appear in an article that otherwise could be useful, although a form of the word or phrase might. If, for example, you are looking for information about gold-plated objects, you should be sure to search for *gold plate, gold plating,* and *gold plated.* Many search tools make this easier by allowing wildcard searches, where a wildcard symbol stands in for one or more other letters. Two commonly used wildcards are the asterisk (*) and question mark (?). With a wildcard, a search for *gold plat** will return pages with the phrases *gold plated*, *gold plating*, and *gold plate* on them.

Other forms of word variants include fused words (*gold plate, goldplate; Web site, Website; e-mail, email; break room, breakroom*) and alternative spellings, especially British and American (*humor, humour; aluminum, aluminium; polyethylene, polythene; theater, theatre; medieval, mediaeval*). To continue with the *gold plate* example, a search might be phrased as *gold plat* OR goldplat** to cover the bases.

- ◆ **Don't forget synonyms.** A synonym is a word with a meaning similar to (not necessarily exactly the same as) another word. For example, *illegal* and *unlawful* are synonyms. If you are writing a paper with the working title "The Illegal Use of Consumer Lasers," you might search on both *illegal laser use* and *unlawful laser use*, because either term might be chosen by an author. A synonym dictionary is a good place to start if you want to find alternate search terms. Once you locate a source or two, you'll find more synonyms there that will help you expand your search. Formal synonyms (*insane, mentally ill*) should usually be preferred over informal ones (*crazy*).

- ◆ **Try related terms.** Related terms are words connected to a subject but not synonymous with each other. For example, The Centers for Medicare and Medicaid Services (www.cms.gov), the government agency that oversees Medicare, is often referred to simply as CMS. If, therefore, you are writing about Medicare, you might want to search on the related term *CMS*.

- ◆ **Explore the Ladder of Generalization.** Words exist along a continuum of specific to general. The more specific, the smaller the group of things covered by the word. For example, the search term *Chihuahua* will return far fewer hits than the term *animal*, because *Chihuahua* is a much more specific word. If you are getting too many hits with your search terms, move down the Ladder of Generalization and use more specific terms. Or, if you are getting too few hits, move up the ladder to more general terms.

Go beyond the Internet

Even though you may be tempted to get all your research information from a Web search, you should expand your efforts. While the Web does contain billions of pages of information, much of it valuable, it still represents a limited source. You will get a much better and more professional picture of your subject by including non-Web sources, especially books and scholarly articles, in your research. You will also develop much better researching skills.

You can perform some beyond-the-Web searching from your computer. Ask a reference librarian which electronic databases are available to you. These databases, such as ProQuest, InfoTrac, EBSCO Host, and JSTOR, feature full-text articles from printed journals. Many public libraries also have some of these databases available to patrons, often accessible from home.

The full text of thousands of books is also available online from various sources (perform a Web search on the phrase "full text books" to find some of these sites). Even though these are older books that are out of copyright, they include such classics as *The Federalist Papers*, Adam Smith's *The Wealth of Nations*, Charles Dickens' *Great Expectations*,

Auguste Comte's *A General View of Positivism*, and many others still useful and pertinent to various research projects.

2.4 Using and abusing Internet sources

The Internet is an amazing grab bag of information, ranging in quality and credibility from excellent to terrible. When you sit down to search the Web, the first thing to remember is that not all information is created equal. Your goal is not merely to find some pages that include your search terms, but to find accurate and reliable information from reputable sources. Cut-and-run searching, where a student grabs whatever comes up on the first page of results, usually produces poor-quality papers. It also teaches students little about the research process.

Search for reliable sites

As you will see in Section 2.5, one of the indicators of the quality of information is its source. We tend to believe those who have knowledge and experience in a subject over those who are expressing the opinion of the day. It is reasonable, then, that organizations specializing in a subject are likely to have better information than a Web page posted by an individual. To begin your topic search, rather than typing in a search phrase and seeing what pages come up, start by looking for sites (that is, organizations) related to your topic. A profitable way to do this is to use your favorite search tool, such as Google or Ask or Yahoo to type in your topic followed by one of these words: *institute, association, forum, foundation, institution.* For example, if you will be writing about peace and conflict in the Middle East, typing in *middle east institute* will return a number of organizations dealing with the Middle East. Try your search topic with each of the other words to locate more organizations.

Another way to locate information from organizations is to use the advanced search commands in the search tool to limit the search results to items in the .org and .gov domains. (The .org domain is for organizations, mostly nonprofit; the .gov domain is for government agencies.)

Look deeply into the results

It is true that the major search engines are constantly tweaking their secret methods of ranking pages so that the best pages appear earliest in the results. However, unlike directories, search engines use computer-based formulas to do the ranking, so many times the pages that you want will be well after the first 10 or 20 displayed by the search tool. Good advice is to (1) craft your search phrase carefully, (2) use more than one phrase, and (3) take the time to look at the first 100 to 200 hits for each query. (Looking at 200 hits might seem like a lot, but it doesn't take as long as you might think.) You can set some of the search engines to return 50 or 100 hits on each page, making scrolling through a large number much more efficient.

Understand the context of individual pages

When you perform a general Web search, do not just grab a page that looks good and use it in your paper. Take some time to discover the context of the page. Try backing up your browser one directory at a time by cutting off each previous directory to see what larger site the page is part of. (Note: If you have the Google toolbar installed in your browser, you can click on the Web *Up* button to go back one folder with each click.)

It may be useful to look at the root Web site of the information, also. On the home page of the root site, you will often find an *About* link that will give you information about the site and its purpose. This may be helpful as you judge the site's quality.

Remember, too, that Web search engines also deliver non-Web sources, such as blog postings. Newsgroup postings range in quality from the word of experts to groundless rantings to intentional falsehoods designed for good or ill (stock price manipulation, for example) to plagiarized pieces of the writings of others. Be very careful to assess the quality of such sources before you make use of them.

Use the invisible Web

A substantial amount of information posted on the Web is not indexed by the search engines. To get to this information on the invisible or deep Web, you must go directly to the various sites that host it. The extra effort needed to access this information is rewarded by the fact that it is usually high in quality.

Many articles from magazines and journals are accessible through the databases on the invisible Web. For example, www.findarticles.com by www.bnet.com features many articles on business and management, and www.magportal.com offers articles from various online publications. Other sites, such as www.completeplanet.com, allow access to many databases not indexed by general search engines such as Google.

Follow the links

Use quality information to find other quality information. When you locate a site or article that you find valuable and credible, visit the links from there to the other information. Not all links are recommendations, of course, but another page deemed worth linking to by a site you find valuable can provide a good possibility for finding more useful and reliable information related to your topic.

2.5 Evaluating sources

Implied above is the idea that sources should be examined for quality before using them. As more and more information becomes available, the range in quality—from treasure to trash—seems to be growing wider. It is increasingly important, then, to apply some effective criteria to the evaluation of each potential source you encounter. Here is one set, known as the EAR test, for Expertise, Accuracy, and Reliability.

Expertise

The first check of a source should relate to the author's credentials. Is the author an authority in the area, an expert, through education, experience, or both? If not, is the author at least well informed about the area and aware of all the relevant issues? If there is a corporate author, is the organization widely respected or an authority? Does the way the author handles the subject indicate that he or she is knowledgeable, reasonable, and a careful thinker? Often, an institutional affiliation will indicate an expert source. For example, a page on the Web site of a chemical manufacturer describing how to mix ingredients to make shampoo should be highly authoritative.

> **The expertise test: Is there evidence that the source knows the subject?**

Accuracy

The next check of a source should relate to accuracy, which includes two parts. First is the currency of the information. Is the information up-to-date? In some areas (technology, business), information becomes outdated rapidly. In other areas (some historical work and literary scholarship), the information remains accurate for long periods. Outdated information can be worse than no information because it can be misleading. Check the date of the source and the date of the information in the source to be sure the information is recent enough for your needs. For example, there was once a concern that LCD televisions could not respond to fast motion quickly enough, resulting in smearing. Reviews of LCD TVs reflected this. Today, after many new generations of LCD TVs, that concern has long been resolved as much faster refresh rates have eliminated smearing. However, some of the older reviews are still online, presenting outdated information.

The second part of accuracy relates to correctness: Are the facts right, are the essential details present, is the presentation unbiased, is the whole picture presented? Be careful of sources that describe everything in sweeping generalizations and that lack details. Sources that ignore conflicting evidence or arguments should be used cautiously, if at all.

The accuracy test: Is the information correct today?

A note on biased sources: There are many areas of controversy, not just in politics, religion, and philosophy, but in science and social science as well, where at least a few of your sources will be somewhat or even highly biased. You can use biased sources, as long as you are aware of the bias and seek out opposing viewpoints (which may be biased as well).

Reliability

The reliability test begins with a look at the source's documentation (bibliography) to see whether the information is well supported. Occasionally, a source will have little documentation because the material is a reasoned argument or a report on an original study or empirical investigation. Usually, though, there will be at least some indication of what other books and articles the authors made use of or recommend for further reading.

Another part of the reliability test concerns how well the information in the source correlates with that in other sources. Corroboration—one source supporting or agreeing with another—is one way to test the credibility of information. The belief is that in matters of fact or data-based conclusions, a source that agrees with other sources is more likely to be correct than a source that does not agree. A good practice, then, is to triangulate your sources: Find three sources that agree on important information. This test is not infallible, for the three sources could be all wrong and the fourth, conflicting source could be correct. Nevertheless, the test is generally a good guideline.

The reliability test: Is the information supported by other sources?

Review questions

To see how well you understand this chapter, attempt to answer each of the following questions without referring to the text. (Write down your answers to make checking easier.) Then check your answers with the text. If you missed something important, add it to your answer.

1. What is the Ladder of Generalization? Give some examples to clarify.

2. In addition to facts, what other kinds of information will be useful to include in a research paper?

3. Distinguish between primary and secondary sources. Give examples.

4. How does quoting a standard dictionary definition weaken a paper?

5. What are some techniques for locating high-quality information on the Internet?

6. Explain the importance of evaluating sources.

Questions for thought and discussion

Use these questions for in-class or small-group discussion, or for stimulating your own thinking.

1. When you write a paper, how do you organize your materials (note cards, data files, folders, etc.)? How effective do you find this method, and why?

2. Have you ever needed to look up a source a second time in order to write down all or part of its bibliographic information? Was it frustrating?

3. How careful are you to think about the wide range of quality and reliability of the information you retrieve from electronic sources? Do you evaluate your sources?

4. When you research, are you more likely to use the first sources you locate, or do you make an attempt to select carefully from a larger set of possibilities? Why?

5. Have you ever written a research paper knowing your position before you began? If so, would you say you were biased? Did any of your research change your opinion?

6. When you finish a paper, what steps do you take to ensure the accuracy of your grammar, spelling, and punctuation?

7. If your school or college has a writing center, have you visited it? What kinds of help did you receive? Did the advice you received improve your paper?

Name _____   Course _____

Chapter 2 Review: True-false quiz

Directions: In each case, determine whether the statement is true or false.

1. The appearance of information in printed form is an indicator of its accuracy.
    ☐ True   ☐ False

2. A source that disagrees with your own conclusions can still be useful.
    ☐ True   ☐ False

3. Everything posted on the Web is indexed by the better search engines.
    ☐ True   ☐ False

4. Reference librarians do not want to be bothered by vague and unfocused questions. Ask them only if you have a specific topic to research.
    ☐ True   ☐ False

5. The Declaration of Independence is an example of a primary source.
    ☐ True   ☐ False

6. The reliability of information sometimes suffers when the primary goal is to make the information entertaining.
    ☐ True   ☐ False

7. Beginning a paper with a quotation from a dictionary is a good way to make a favorable impression on your reader.
    ☐ True   ☐ False

8. An important consideration for the EAR (Expertise, Accuracy, and Reliability) test of source evaluation is whether or not there is a date on a Web page you might use.
    ☐ True   ☐ False

9. Because you are writing for your instructor, you really don't need to think about your audience and how best to meet your audience's needs.
    ☐ True   ☐ False

10. Carefully taken lecture notes can be used as a source in a research paper.
    ☐ True   ☐ False

3
Preparing Your Sources

Pale ink is better than the most retentive memory.
—Confucius

In this chapter, you will learn to work with the sources you have selected to prepare them for use in your paper. In the reading and note-taking phase of your research project, you should begin to identify which information you want to use in your paper. As you read and think about each source you have selected, take notes about important points and then choose passages for possible quotation, paraphrase, or summary. This chapter emphasizes the practical habits that will help you keep your research materials and notes under control.

- ♦ Collecting and organizing your sources carefully will make working with them much easier.
- ♦ Taking careful notes on the first reading will save rereading time later on, and make using information from the source more efficient and accurate.
- ♦ Protecting your writing and research work will help you avoid a false charge of plagiarism.

3.1 Collecting sources

Potentially, the most frustrating part of writing a research paper is losing track of a source. You may have a great quotation that brilliantly sums up your major point, only to discover that you have lost the record of where you got it. Or, you may have the source, but note that you neglected to write down the entire bibliographical entry, meaning another trip to the library or another search on the database. These oversights are all too common: Listen to the voice of experience and save yourself much effort by following these guidelines:

Photocopy, print, or save your sources

As you locate each useful source, make a personal copy of it. Articles from printed journals can be photocopied; pages from chapters of books can also be photocopied; articles from the Web or electronic databases can be saved and printed out. The doctrine of *fair use* under United States copyright law allows you to make a photocopy of a copyrighted article for personal use in scholarly work such as writing a research paper.

Why should you do this? There are several reasons:

- ♦ **A copy keeps the context.** A full copy of an article or section of a book lets you see the quotation or information in context. As you think through the information, the context may cause you to rethink your initial interpretation.
- ♦ **A copy is a handy source.** You can return to the source easily any time you want. You will not need to look it up again or revisit the library. As you write your paper, new ideas or a change in the direction of your central idea might

cause you to return to a source and use something different or additional. The convenience of having the source always at hand cannot be overstated.

- **A copy can be written on.** On a hardcopy, you can write notes, highlight passages, fold down corners, or whatever else helps you process and use the source. Reading an article online or in a printed journal and only making notes (whether handwritten or typed) is much less effective for most students than making copies and writing on them.

- **A copy is an easy reference.** Just before turning in the paper, you can double-check the accuracy of the quotations, the spelling of names or technical terms, and the correctness of numbers and other information.

- **Copies might be required.** Many instructors require annotated copies of sources to be turned in with rough drafts or with the final draft of the research paper.

- **Copies can help establish authorship.** Source copies (especially marked-up source copies) provide evidence that will help defend you in the event you are falsely accused of plagiarism.

Get the full, exact bibliographic information the first time

This advice seems to be obvious. However, experience shows that many times, especially with journal articles, students write down only the pages from which they quote and neglect to write down the beginning and ending pages (as in 126-142) required for the Works Cited or References page. The result is that these students must look up the source again, making another trip to the library or duplicating a search on a database.

If you follow the advice about photocopying your sources, be sure that you photocopy the title page of any books you use. Because the copyright date is usually on the reverse side of the title page, write that date on the photocopied title page. Similarly, photocopy the cover or contents page of all journals, being sure you get the journal title, date, and volume information. When you photocopy an article, be sure that page numbers are clearly visible on each page. If not, write the correct ones on the pages before you leave the library.

A FAVORITE FILE

If you are researching Web articles on your own PC, each time you find a useful item, add it to your saved links (Favorites, Bookmarks, etc.) in your browser. If you are researching on school computers, open a word processing document and copy and paste the URL from each source you locate. Either method will make returning to the source later on much easier.

For Web and electronic database sources, copy and paste the full URL (uniform resource locator—the Web address) from the location window to a file. When a Web page prints out, many of the URLs are too long to include on the printed page, so they are truncated, leaving you with only a partial address. Unless the URL is clearly short and prints out in its entirety on the page, be sure to copy it while you have the article on the screen. If you need to go back to the source, you will have the address handy.

Note: Do not use the URL from Web shortening services (bit.ly, Tiny URL, goo.gl, etc.) because those URLs represent redirected addresses rather than the actual address of the source page.

Photographs, graphics, charts, tables, drawings, and other visual information taken from the Web present a special problem because when you save them to a file as individual graphic files, the URLs are not included. Take care, therefore, to note the URL of the graphic when you save it. A good practice is to print the page or article containing the graphic so that you have both the graphic in context and the URL of the source page. At the least, paste each graphic into a word processing file and include the URL of the source beneath the graphic. And it's a good idea to include some notes explaining the significance of the graphic and how you plan to use it in your paper.

3.2 Keep sources organized

If you make printouts and photocopies of your sources (even the ones you save to a file from electronic databases), you can keep them organized by putting them in a binder. Data files can be organized on a flash drive or other storage medium. As you read through your sources and begin to see where they might be used in your paper, consider using divider tabs to collect the sources in relevant sections.

In addition to a printout of your electronic sources, you will benefit by saving them in data files. If you copy and paste your quotations from a file version of an article, the quotation will be exact and there will be none of the copying errors that can occur with hand copying. It's all too easy to miss a word (like *not*) or to skip a line when typing out a quotation from a printed source. An additional advantage of a file version of the information is that you can highlight a section of the source and then add a bracketed note in the file, indicating where in your paper you used the information. For example, "[This section quoted in the second paragraph on Mnemonics]."

Be sure that your paper includes an accurate reference to the source for each copy-and-paste quotation.

Start a bibliography

Rather than jot down haphazardly the author and title of each work you have located, start your bibliography with the first work you find. You will eventually need to create a Works Cited page for an MLA-style paper or a References page for an APA-style paper, so why not begin now, enter the first source in the proper format, and add each new source to it as you find it?

The running bibliography serves you in several ways. First, it helps you keep track of all your sources in one place for quick, easy reference. It will immediately answer questions such as, "Did I already look at this source?" "Was the study by Jenkins published before or after the experiment by Smervits?" or even, "Am I drawing too much [or too little] on Web [or book or journal] sources, or in some other way not meeting the research requirements for the paper?"

Another benefit to keeping an up-to-date bibliography is that it's much easier to enter each new source alphabetically and in proper format, one at a time, than it is to locate, organize, and enter the entire dozen or two or three sources at the end of your project, when some early references might be buried somewhere—or missed altogether.

31

3.3 Take careful notes

A major source of confusion, inaccuracy—and sometimes plagiarism—lies in improper note-taking practices. Students who include quotations, summaries, paraphrases, and their own analyses in their reading notes, without clearly distinguishing among those different kinds of information, create difficulties for themselves. If you haven't already had the experience, you will be surprised how confusing notes can be once you leave them for a day or two and come back to work with them—unless you practice careful note-taking behavior. Following are some suggestions that will enable you to take careful notes.

Use a labeling system

Make use of a system for labeling the various kinds of notes you write down: quotations, comments by you, paraphrases, or summaries. Then, when you are making notes as you read a book or an article, apply the technique as you read. The goal is to distinguish clearly what each note represents. These distinctions will also enable you to work more quickly because the meaning of each note will always be clear.

- **Include the full bibliographic citation** at the beginning of your notes so that subsequent references can be by author and page number or some other shortened format. See Examples 3.3.1 and 3.3.2 below.

- **Use quotation marks around all word-for-word copying**, and include a clear citation. If you take notes by hand, use a large, exaggerated size for the quotation marks to make them clearly visible. In a word processing document, you can insert a symbol such as this one of a speaking man to indicate that these words are directly from the source. For the sake of clear note taking, put in the quotation marks even for long quotations that might later become block quotations in your paper (without quotation marks). It's always easier to remove a pair of quotation marks than it is to wonder whether a passage is a quotation or your own work.

- **Label paraphrases with a circled *P*** or other distinguishing mark. When you turn the text into your own words in a paraphrase, you may at a later time confuse it with your own ideas unless it is clearly labeled. Include a citation. A symbol from those available in your word processor can be used for marking paraphrases in document files.

- **Label summaries with a circled *S*** or other distinguishing mark or symbol. Summaries reduce the material to a shorter form in your own words, so they are even more likely than paraphrases to be confused with your own work unless they are clearly labeled. Once again, remember to include a citation. Instead of a circled S for marking summaries in a word processing document, you might use another symbol, such as the lightning bolt (to symbolize the electrifying core meaning?).

- **Label your own ideas with the word *Mine*** or other mark or symbol. When you add commentary, analysis, or simply write down an idea that occurred to you as you read, circle that writing and attach a label. Your ideas are valuable. Protect them. For the word processing file, the symbol here is the circled *i*, normally standing for information, but in this case the research paper writer uses it to mean "my idea."

♦ **The labeling system you use can be your own**, and it can use any letters or symbols (or colors or fonts) you want, as long as you are consistent and the system is meaningful to you. (The symbols above are all Webdings found in Microsoft Word.)

Example 3.3.1
Sample Notes
Quoted text with bibliographic citation: book, APA style:
Doe, J. (2007). *Tracking subatomic particles*. New York: Physics Press.
👤 "The question remains: Are quarks the fundamental building blocks of matter, or is there something smaller?" middle of page 261
👤 "There are perhaps 100 quintillion atoms in a grain of sand, and yet matter is mostly space." very bottom of page 144

Quoted text with bibliographic citation: book, MLA style:
Doe, John. *Tracking Subatomic Particles*. New York: Physics Press, 2007.
👤 "The question remains: Are quarks the fundamental building blocks of matter, or is there something smaller?" middle of page 261
👤 "There are perhaps 100 quintillion atoms in a grain of sand, and yet matter is mostly space." very bottom of page 144

Example 3.3.2
Sample Notes
Quoted text with bibliographic citation: article, APA style:
Doe, J. (2009). "A new test for blood evidence." *Journal of Forensic Science, 22*, 265-274.
👤 "The use of Luminol can be problematic because it can produce false positives for blood and damage real blood." three lines from bottom of page 266

Quoted text with bibliographic citation: article, MLA style:
Doe, Jane. "A New Test for Blood Evidence." *Journal of Forensic Science* 22 (2009): 265-74.
👤 "The use of Luminol can be problematic because it can produce false positives for blood and damage real blood." three lines from bottom of page 266

Comment:
Note that the bibliographic citation for the article includes the beginning and ending page numbers of the article.

If you take notes by hand, you can be creative by using different ink colors to distinguish among the kinds of notes (such as red for quotations, green for paraphrases, blue for summaries, and black for your own ideas), or you can draw boxes or shapes around the text and add labels. If you take notes on a computer, you can use different fonts, different colors of text, or boxes and labels to mark the different kinds of information. Not only do you want to be careful to identify and give credit to your source when you use it, but *you also want to be sure that you do not accidentally give your source credit for your own thinking. Your ideas are important.*

Add purpose comments or indicators to your notes

Whether you put individual notes on note cards or in word processing files, a good strategy is to indicate the category grouping or orientation of each note. That is, describe briefly how the note (quotation, summary, paraphrase, your own comment) might fit into your structure. Does the note provide background or contextual information, support a theory, rebut a claim, provide statistics for or against a conclusion, or belong to a particular theoretical or interpretive camp? When you later assemble your sources for use, these grouping labels and comments will enable you to arrange them more easily.

As your research progresses, you will begin to get a feel for how your sources might be arranged. When you are far enough along, you can begin to add organizational comments to your notes. See the bracketed comment in the example below, where the student has tentatively suggested the connection between two sources.

> **Example 3.3.3**
> Sample Note
> Johnson, "Asynchronous," 343-45 >>>PRO asynchronous
> ✎ ✇ Johnson believes that asynchronous interactions can be more beneficial to the student than real-time (live or distant) ones, because "many otherwise shy learners are emboldened by the protected arena of offline communication." 345 [Put after Jackson's criticism? Jackson, "Learning Modes," 298]
> ⓘ Johnson focuses on student willingness to ask the professor questions in e-mail, but doesn't cover threaded discussion groups. This may be a weakness to his argument.
>
> Comment:
> In this Sample Note, the researcher identifies the source briefly ("Johnson, Asynchronous"). The student keeps a running bibliography, so the full citation is not needed for each note. The page numbers indicate the range of the article or book being referred to in the note (here, partially summarized and partially quoted, as the symbols indicate). The marker ">>>PRO asynchronous" is a category grouping, telling the researcher that this note contains information that favors asynchronous learning. The bracketed comment at the end is an early thought by the researcher about how the source might eventually fit into the paper. And the researcher's own analysis or commentary is identified by the symbol ⓘ, so that it is clearly distinguishable from the source.

Quote exactly

If you are working with physical documents, where you must transcribe the words by handwriting, typing, or even scanning using optical character recognition software, there is a chance for errors to enter the text. Even copying and pasting from an electronic source can introduce errors, especially at the beginning and end of the quotation, because words or punctuation marks are sometimes cut off. Double-check to assure that the text has been copied accurately—that all the words, including proper names, are spelled correctly and that no words have been left out. The word *not* is commonly left out when copying manually, and the loss of that word obviously has a critical effect on the meaning of a quotation.

Quoting exactly also means that you are not permitted to change the spelling of any words in the source, even if that spelling is archaic, incorrect, or nonstandard. For example, you may encounter British spellings such as *humour, honour,* or *aluminium.* In such a case, follow the text. If there is an error in your source text, where a word has been left out, do not silently correct the text. You may insert a missing word with brackets [like this]. In the situation where you encounter a typographical error, you must still quote the source exactly, and then indicate that you are indeed transcribing verbatim by adding the word *sic* in brackets. See Chapter 4, Section 4.4 for additional information.

KEEP A QUOTATION FILE

One of the most common reasons given for inadvertent plagiarism is "confusion in my notes." In other words, because of poor note-taking control, the writer mixed up quoted material with the writer's own words and, when it was time to draft the paper, the writer was unable to see the difference, resulting in plagiarizing the quoted material.

A good way to help protect yourself from this problem is to keep a separate word processing file for quotations that you copy from electronic sources such as the Web or electronic databases. When you use the quoted material, copy it from your file and paste it into your paper (with appropriate citation, of course). By doing that, if there is ever any question about the quotation (or paraphrase or summary, or your notes and comments about it), you can look back at the original and make the comparison easily.

A separate file for each source makes organizing quotations easy, and it allows you to enter the full bibliographic citation only once at the top of the file, and then use a short reference in subsequent notes. (See the difference between Example 3.3.2 with a full citation and Example 3.3.3 with a brief reference.)

Keep copies of each source with your notes

Stapling a printout or photocopy of a source article or book pages to the back of your notes about the source will keep the source handy for further reference, for last-minute triple-checking of quotations, and for referring to any notes you made in the margins as you read. The printout includes the context of the words around your quotation or other reference, so that you can recheck that your interpretation or other comment is based on an accurate understanding of the source. Further research and thinking may also lead you to use more of the source than you originally planned. In such a case, the entire source is handy. (If you do not keep a copy of a source and have to return to it later, you may need to read the entire article again because you will not be able to rely on the annotations you made earlier.)

Archive your notes

As you work with your sources and notes, do not throw anything away. When you are finished with a source, put your notes and the copy of the source in a notebook and hold on to it. If your notes are in electronic form and you use them as a source for copying and pasting, or if you add to and delete as you work toward your final paper, keep copies of printouts or copies of earlier versions of your data files. If any confusion should arise—over what is a quotation and what is your own thinking, for example— you will have the earlier version available to you for consultation and clarification. Early versions of notes may also be useful if you decide to change direction in the paper. And, of course, your ability to demonstrate a history of work on your paper will help protect you from a false charge of plagiarism.

3.4 Protect yourself against a false charge of plagiarism

If you need proof of the value of someone's writing as intellectual property, take note of the fact that student research papers are now being stolen and sold or traded to others (both on campus and on the Web). Imagine your dismay if you, as an honest student, work hard to produce a great research paper, only to be confronted by your instructor, who says that your paper is available on the Web or has been flagged as containing plagiarism by a commercial plagiarism service. Following are several steps you can take to protect yourself from a problem like this.

Protect your data and passwords

An individual research paper can require dozens of hours of work; the papers you have completed in a typical year can therefore represent hundreds of hours of mental effort. If they are saved on a CD-R or flash memory stick, they are neatly packaged and handy for any thief. Even printouts require only a few minutes to scan and convert back into electronic format ready for editing and a false claim of authorship by a thief.

To those who would like to skip the labor but get the credit for it, your work is a valuable commodity. Your stolen papers could be turned in by the thief, sold to another student, or uploaded to a paper mill Web site in trade for another paper. Therefore, whatever storage method you use—printout, CD-R, flash memory stick, your PC's hard drive, a network drive, an external USB or Firewire hard drive, a Web storage service, or some other medium—be certain that you keep your work secure from potential thieves.

A final way to protect your paper is to ask your instructor not to return papers by putting them outside his or her office on a chair or in a rack. You might be finished with your paper, but a thief might be just beginning to work with it.

Do not lend, give, or upload any paper

Many professors wish they had a dollar for every time they have heard of a student who lent a paper to another student "to look at" or "for reference," only to have that other student turn the paper in, claiming to have written it. If your paper is turned in by someone else, you may be accused of being an accessory to plagiarism. At the very least, you should not want your work to be stolen in that way.

As mentioned above, another risk now is that if you lose possession of your paper, it may be uploaded to a mill site in trade for another paper or simply as a gift to others. Should your professor search the Web and locate your paper on a mill site, you may be accused of having downloaded it from the site.

Be wise, therefore, and remember that lending your flash drive, e-mailing your paper, giving out your password, letting a friend use your computer, or even lending a printout puts you at great risk. If you are persuaded to let a friend look at one of your papers, show it while you are present, if possible. Once the paper is out of your sight, you cannot know what might happen to it.

Report any theft immediately

Should you know or believe that one or more of your papers might have been stolen or otherwise compromised, report that fact immediately. If a paper you are working on or have just handed in is stolen, inform the instructor in the class for which it is due. If the term has ended, you should still report the theft, either to the instructor, the department, a dean, or other authority as soon as you discover the theft. (Waiting until you are accused of plagiarism to claim that your paper was stolen looks like a last-minute excuse.) Ask one of your instructors about institutional policy for reporting theft after a term has ended.

Save and print all drafts and notes

Take a moment to imagine that you are an instructor grading research papers. You read one that is very good. Just to be cautious, you check for the paper on the Web, and to your surprise, you find it on a mill site. You call in the student who handed in the paper. "Did you really write this paper?" you ask. "Yes," says the student. "Okay," you say, "show me your rough drafts." "I threw them all away," the student replies. After this exchange, would you be more suspicious of the authorship or less?

Whatever your answer, you should be able to see that a good way to protect yourself from a false charge of plagiarism is to keep all the evidence that you really did write the paper: the note cards, printouts, drafts, scratch outlines, or whatever else you may have. Good advice is to *print out the current draft of your paper each time you work on it* so that you will have a printed record of its various stages of creation. Whether you follow this advice and print it out or not, at least save each draft under a new file name after each editing session. Keep copies in two secure locations in case one is lost or destroyed. Hard disk drives crash and network storage sometimes loses data.

Imagine once again that you are an instructor. In looking over your grades, you notice that you have no grade for Jane's paper. You see her in class. "Jane, why didn't you turn in a paper?" you ask. "I did turn one in," Jane says. "Well," you say, "I didn't get it or I lost it. Bring me another copy tomorrow." "I can't," Jane tells you, "because I lost my USB drive." "Don't you have a copy of the paper?" you ask. "No," she answers.

What would you do in a circumstance like this? If you do what many instructors do, Jane will have to write another paper and possibly take a late penalty. Once again, do not underestimate the value of your work. Protect all those hours of work by keeping multiple copies in safe places.

Photocopy or print out and save all sources

In addition to the drafts and working notes, among the most convincing evidence that you have written a paper are photocopies of all the sources you used, nicely marked with ink or highlighter as you read through them and organized quotations or other references for use in your paper. If you can put photocopied pages and Web printouts on your instructor's desk and say, "Here are the sources of my quotations," in two minutes, you will most likely clear yourself of any accusation that you downloaded the paper.

Because Web sites can change unpredictably, it is especially important to print out the material you use (or save the pages to a file). Journal articles from online databases should be printed out, while journal articles in print form can be photocopied. For books, photocopy only the title page and the pages you actually cite (whether you quote, paraphrase, summarize, or only refer to them). And, as mentioned before, get the copyright information from the verso (back side) of the title page. Sometimes the information includes edition or reprint information that is as important for your bibliography as the copyright date.

More and more instructors are requiring these copies of sources to be made and submitted with the final version of the research paper. Even if copies are not required, however, they provide inexpensive insurance, as well as an excellent resource during the writing of your paper.

SAVE THAT WEB PAGE

Many popular Web browsers have the ability to save Web pages, with all their added graphics and hyperlinked content, in a single file for later viewing offline. Internet Explorer and Opera can save Web pages in .mht format, and Safari can save them in .webarchive format. An alternative is to convert the page to a .pdf document using one of the many converters available.

Be proactive

As you work on your paper, visit your instructor to ask for input and feedback. Input involves asking the instructor's advice about research strategies (such as where to look, what keywords to use, what sources are recommended, or what direction to pursue with your topic). Early on, feedback involves discussing the central idea you plan to support; later, it may include showing your instructor preliminary sections of the paper in order to ensure that you are fulfilling the requirements and are generally on the right track.

When you have a substantial draft, visit the writing center for help with structure or style (or even grammar and mechanics). Keep the marked-up draft. (Some writing centers have a stamp or require their tutors to sign drafts or pages of comments. If your center has such a policy, keep this evidence of your visit.) Feedback on drafts (from the instructor and the writing center) also provides you with the opportunity to be sure that you are incorporating sources properly and not inadvertently plagiarizing any of them. Be specific in your interest here, telling your instructor or tutor that you are concerned that all your sources receive proper acknowledgment.

To add unique content to your work, conduct your own survey to gather opinions about an aspect of your subject, or call or e-mail an expert for an interview. Perform an experiment or collect your own data by measuring or counting something relevant to your topic. (If you meet with your instructor for feedback, ask about a useful experiment or survey that you might perform.)

All of these steps will make your paper much better, and they will also establish a construction trail demonstrating that you have worked on the paper well in advance of the due date.

Review questions

To see how well you understand this chapter, attempt to answer each of the following questions without referring to the text. (Write down your answers to make checking easier.) Then check your answers with the text. If you missed something important, add it to your answer.

1. What are the benefits of having printed copies of each source?

2. Why should you archive your notes as you construct your research paper?

3. What does it mean to add comments to your notes, and why is it useful?

4. Describe some of the ways you can protect yourself against a false charge of plagiarism.

Questions for thought and discussion

Use these questions for in-class or small-group discussion, or for stimulating your own thinking.

1. Has this chapter encouraged you to adopt the advice about note taking and source preparation? If so, which suggestions have you chosen to follow, and why?

2. As you take notes, how do you make sure to identify the difference between a quotation and a summary or between a quotation and your own ideas? (In other words, what kind of note-taking system do you use?)

3. Have you ever been told by an instructor that your paper was lost? Did you have a copy? What happened?

4. Have you ever been asked to lend your paper to someone "just to look at"? What did you do? What will you do in the future? Why?

Name _____   Course _____

Chapter 3 Review: True-false quiz

Directions: In each case, determine whether the statement is true or false.

1. When working with sources, using a labeling system can help distinguish not only between a quotation and a paraphrase, but also between a source's idea and your own.
   ☐ True   ☐ False

2. Printing or copying sources makes working with them easier because you can write on, highlight, and keep them handy.
   ☐ True   ☐ False

3. There is no reason to keep the drafts of your research paper after you turn it in.
   ☐ True   ☐ False

4. When you make a note on a source, you can include information about the general category or position the source takes, and you can add your own comments.
   ☐ True   ☐ False

5. An important reason for distinguishing carefully between your source's words or ideas and your own is to make sure that you do not accidentally give your source credit for your own thinking.
   ☐ True   ☐ False

6. When collecting and preparing sources, it is best to wait to create your bibliography until after you have all your sources in hand.
   ☐ True   ☐ False

7. If a source misspells a word in a quotation you want to use, you can silently correct it so that your instructor will not think you made a mistake.
   ☐ True   ☐ False

8. A good way to make sure you quote an electronically available source exactly is to copy and paste it rather than type it in from a printout or handwritten notes.
   ☐ True   ☐ False

9. Student research papers are marketable commodities and can be in danger of theft by opportunists.
   ☐ True   ☐ False

10. Visiting the writing center or performing your own survey or experiment can help you establish authorship of your work if it is challenged later on.
    ☐ True   ☐ False

4
Quoting Effectively

I quote others only to express myself better.
—Michel de Montaigne

In this chapter, you will learn the art of effective quotation, together with many useful techniques that add focus, emphasis, and variety to your use of quoted sources. The ideas presented here will add a number of tools to your writing toolkit, which in turn will allow you to present quotations with more refinement.

+ Learning about the uses of quotation will help you choose when to quote.
+ Understanding how quotations can become ineffective or even fallacious will protect you against these pitfalls.
+ Using a variety of introductory strategies will improve your reader's interest in and engagement with the sources you quote.
+ Choosing appropriate quoting strategies will make your writing clearer and more effective.

4.1 Quoting use and abuse

Using a quotation—someone's exact words—can have a dramatic and powerful effect in your paper, for you are displaying verbatim (word for word) what someone, often an expert, has said about the point you are making.

When to choose quotation

Direct quotation may be preferable to a summary or paraphrase for any of several reasons. A few of the unique benefits offered by a direct quotation are as follows:

+ **Expert declaration.** The exact words of an authority are more powerful than a summary or paraphrase of those words, even if the exact words are not remarkable in themselves. When readers can see precisely what an expert says, they can analyze, dwell on, or react to those words without any concern that some meaning has been lost through a paraphrase or summary.
+ **Direct support.** An effective way to reinforce a point you are making is to supply a quotation that provides support for it. Quotations have a sense of presence or immediacy that paraphrases or summaries lack. The quotation serves as a second voice, seemingly speaking now, confirming your point.
+ **Effective language.** The quality of the writer's language may make it highly quotable. Its elegance, clarity, directness, use of metaphor or other imagery, exactness, aptness—any of these may make the words worth quoting because they will add interest to your paper. Having another voice enter the discussion provides variety as well as impact. If the source says something better than you could, consider quoting.

◆ **Historical flavor.** If you make use of a source from many years ago, the style and vocabulary (and even the spelling) may allow a quotation to offer a special zest to your paper. Some writers have a distinctive and commanding style or an engaging use of rhetorical flourish that offers a unique feel to their ideas.

◆ **Specific example.** A source may tell a story, supply an anecdote, or offer a vivid example best presented in the source's own words. Because most anecdotes are condensed and carefully sequenced, they are almost impossible to paraphrase or summarize without losing their snap or even their meaning.

◆ **Controversial statement.** If the source makes an outrageous or highly controversial claim, quoting the source directly will (1) remove your reader's skepticism about what the source really said and (2) help distance you from responsibility for the idea or the words used to express it.

◆ **Material for analysis.** When you intend to comment on, explain, analyze, or criticize an idea, quoting it places the exact words at issue before the reader for reference as you make your remarks. You can then proceed to quote short phrases or even single words in your analysis without confusing the reader about the context of those words.

Cautions about quoting

If wisdom is the prudent application of knowledge, then use wisdom when you decide to quote. Here are three unwise uses of quotation:

◆ **Quoting too often.** Too many quotations in a paper will push your ideas into the background and take over the paper, rather than act as a support to your writing. Remember that your own thinking is the purpose of the paper; you are not assembling a quotation dictionary. If you explain, discuss, or apply most of your quotations, you should be able to avoid overquotation. The number of quotations considered too many depends upon the nature of the writing project, of course, but it also depends upon how long the quotations are. Quotations can range from fairly long to very short. As a rule, short quotations can appear more frequently than long quotations.

◆ **Quoting one source too many times.** Some instructors provide rules of thumb for their research paper assignments, not permitting the quotation (or citation in any form) of one source more than a certain number of times. (For example, the rule may be that a student may not use one source more than three times in a 2,500-word paper.) Whether you have such a rule or not, the overuse of one source implies too much dependence on it. If the citations from a single source occur one after the other without other intervening citations, and if they are sequential (as in pages 265, 288, and 299), it will appear to the reader that the source is being transferred into the paper wholesale, rather than being integrated and analyzed along with other materials.

◆ **Quoting too long.** For many instructors, a synonym for *lengthy quotation* is *padding* because in many cases that is exactly what is taking place. However, there is another reason for avoiding lengthy quotations: They are ineffective. Many readers have a habit of skipping past long quotations. An occasional four- to six-line quotation might be desirable, but a ten- or twelve-line quotation would need to be quite spectacular to be worth including.

Avoid the fallacy of vicious abstraction

Vicious abstraction occurs when a quotation takes on a meaning different from that intended by its author because the words are taken out of their surrounding context. Vicious abstraction can occur as a result of several different circumstances:

♦ **The source author is presenting someone else's position.** Many writers summarize or paraphrase their opponent's position by speaking in the voice of the opponent in order to be fair and to add realism. Recognizing when the writer is presenting another's ideas is important because the writer is merely *describing* those views, not *advocating* them. If a research paper writer quotes from one of these summaries and attributes the views to the source writer, vicious abstraction results.

♦ **The source author's words require the source context** for an accurate understanding of the meaning, and quoting the words out of context creates a false impression. Many statements require some context (such as the surrounding paragraph) in order to be fully and accurately understood.

♦ **The research paper writer omits some words from the quotation** (often clearly showing the omission with ellipsis dots), and the abbreviated quotation takes on a meaning different from the full quotation. You are allowed to omit words from a quotation for the sake of eliminating unnecessary language, but the meaning of the quotation must remain the same.

Example 4.1.1

Quotation:

The group known as Motorists for Faster Driving argues that higher speed limits will enable us to get to our destinations faster, thus reducing our risk time on the road. In other words, we should raise or eliminate speed limits for safety's sake. Such an argument neglects the fact that higher speed equals higher-speed crashes. —John Doe, 2006, p. 75

Vicious abstraction, MLA style:

John Doe believes that "we should raise or eliminate speed limits for safety's sake" (75).

Comment:

While the words are accurately quoted from Doe, they represent a viewpoint he is describing (and then rejecting) rather than one he is advocating.

Example 4.1.2

Quotation:

A little learning is a dang'rous thing;
Drink deep, or taste not the Pierian spring:
There shallow draughts intoxicate the brain,
And drinking largely sobers us again.
—Alexander Pope

Vicious abstraction:

Alexander Pope warns us that "learning is a dang'rous thing."

Comment:

Pope's point is that a small amount of learning is dangerous, but that great learning "sobers us" and is thus beneficial. The vicious abstraction expresses nearly the opposite idea.

43

Example 4.1.3
Quotation:
It is unfortunate that the small sample and the questionable quality of the data leave this theory completely unsupported. The theory is plausible and provocative. The experimental design is excellent, and if—and only if—Jones and Brown can supply a new, reliable data set with the same outcome, the results will revolutionize the way we view the brain.
—Jane Doe, 2008, p. 456

Vicious abstraction, APA style:
Jane Doe (2008) affirmed the discipline-changing impact of the Jones and Brown findings: "The theory is plausible and provocative. The experimental design is excellent, and . . . the results will revolutionize the way we view the brain" (p. 456).

Comment:
By omitting the strong conditional "if" statement, as well as the context supplied by Doe's criticism of the data and its implications, the writer here has presented a completely misleading representation of Doe's position, *even though every word quoted is accurate.*

Whenever you draw upon a source, then, quoting or otherwise, be very careful that you preserve the source's real meaning. Never attempt to make a source say what you want it to say. If you think that a source is wrong, criticize it robustly, but don't distort the author's meaning.

4.2 Introductory strategies

One function of introducing quotations is to mark clearly for the reader the boundary between your discussion and the use of research material. Even a simple introductory lead-in not only serves to honor the idea of intellectual property and prevent plagiarism (see Chapter 7 on marking the boundaries), but it also helps your reader to understand how the source information fits into the argument of your paper.

Introduce your sources

If you could be a fly on the wall of a coffeehouse, and if you could land near a table of instructors, you might hear the way they describe quotations that appear suddenly and unannounced in a paper: "disembodied quotations," "phantom words," "ghost quotations," "unannounced strangers." Rather than making a sudden and unexpected appearance, quotations should be introduced in some way that helps the reader prepare for them. The introductory lead-in provides an informational hook or a micro-context that lets the reader know a little about what is coming.

An introductory lead-in can include one or more of the following elements:

- ◆ **The author's name**
  - ◆ According to Doe,
  - ◆ John Doe writes that
  - ◆ In an article by John Doe, we read
- ◆ **A description of the author** (credentials, job title, etc.)
  - ◆ A Yale University psychologist reported
  - ◆ A State of California geologist says

- ◆ A researcher who specializes in radiometric dating concludes
- ◆ **The title of the book or article**
  - ◆ In *A History of Secret Codes*, we learn
  - ◆ The article, "The Botanical Source of Western Medicine," traces
  - ◆ *Quantum Mechanics for Dummies* surveys
- ◆ **The name of the journal or Web site**
  - ◆ A study of the poet first appeared in *English Renaissance History*, discussing
  - ◆ The Institute for Strategic Management Web site offers information about
  - ◆ The *Journal of Polymer Chemistry* surveyed
- ◆ **A brief summary of the content**
  - ◆ In a discussion of the relationship between chocolate consumption and depression,
  - ◆ A rhetorical analysis of the poem has shown
  - ◆ A recent article about the design of room lighting tells us
- ◆ **An expression of the role of the quotation**
  - ◆ Arguing exactly the opposite,
  - ◆ Support for this view comes from
  - ◆ Coming to a similar conclusion by way of a different approach,
- ◆ **A combination of the above elements** (two or three at most)
  - ◆ Too many words, argues Jane Doe, can obscure meaning:
  - ◆ John Doe, writing in the *Journal of Numismatics and Philatelics*, notes that many people collect for both esthetic and investment reasons:
  - ◆ A report by a water analysis laboratory names the probable source:

Use a variety of introductory verbs

"John Doe says" is always one way to introduce a quotation, of course. However, using the same introductory verb over and over will get old quickly. Choosing a variety of verbs will keep your writing from appearing mechanical. Another reason for using different verbs is that a carefully chosen one will help set up the quotation by giving your reader an indication of the role of the quotation. "John Doe shows" provides very different guidance from "John Doe objects."

Use the appropriate tense in your introductory phrases for APA style

In the examples in this book, the tense of the introductory verbs includes both present and past, to show you the possibilities. And later in this section, you will learn about historical present tense. MLA style allows great flexibility in choosing the tense of introductory verbs. However, APA style requires a much more structured and specific use of tense.

For APA, use past tense when reporting events or actions from a specific time in the past, such as research studies, experiments, or writing. This applies to reporting about your own work and that of others.

- ◆ Doe (2010) reported that this was the case.
- ◆ The experiment found that few subjects were able to transfer the analogy to the problem.

- Doe and Smith (2008) discovered some additional instances of the phenomenon.
- In a paper presented in early 2003, Doe hypothesized that A did, in fact, cause B.
- We tested the hearing of 36 subjects to determine the highest frequency they could hear.
- Volunteers distributed to shoppers what appeared to be valuable coupons.
- In an earlier version of this experiment, we sampled 18 brands of razor.
- Our experiment studied the behavior of an entirely different group.

Use present perfect tense to report events or actions that occurred at a nonspecific time in the past or that occurred over time in the past.

- Others have duplicated these findings.
- Some have replicated these or similar experiments.
- Other studies have shown an even larger impact.
- Several researchers investigating this phenomenon have found further evidence of statistical error.
- This hypothesis has resulted in an ongoing debate about the origin of the phenomenon.

Use present tense to reflect current belief, implications, ideas, or conclusions about the results of research.

- This research appears to show that reading too much at once increases forgetfulness.
- There are several competing hypotheses that explain the data nearly as well.
- Most of the available evidence argues for the conclusion that odors are keenly connected to memory.
- We conclude, therefore, that the phenomenon presents itself whenever noise levels exceed 90 decibels.

Note how these tenses can be combined.

- Doe and Smith (2010) designed four experiments whose conclusions support the hypothesis that practicing creative thinking techniques improves creativity.
- Several historical studies (e.g., Doe & Smith, 2006; Jones, 2008; Brown & Johnson, 2009) have shown that the two effects seldom appear together.
- In an experiment on mice, Doe (2001) concluded that high-voltage shocks from cattle prods inhibit the curiosity of mice.

The table, Introductory Verbs, on the facing page offers a number of choices for you. The list is not exhaustive, but it will begin your thinking about the kinds of verbs you can use and the various ways you can prepare your reader for the role of the quotation in your paper. The verbs are all in present tense, so that if you are writing a paper in APA style, you will need to change them to past or present perfect tense as appropriate to meet APA requirements.

INTRODUCTORY VERBS

Says
The verb introduces the quotation as information.

adds	mentions
believes	notes
clarifies	observes
comments	offers
describes	points out
discusses	remarks
emphasizes	reports
examines	reveals
explains	says
explores	states
identifies	writes

Agrees
The verb indicates that the source agrees with another source or with the position you are advancing.

accepts	concurs
agrees	parallels
assents	supports

Yields
The source agrees that a conflicting point is valid.

acknowledges	concedes
admits	grants
agrees	recognizes
allows	

Argues in favor
The verb indicates that the source is providing evidence or reasons for a position.

argues	indicates
asserts	insists
contends	maintains
demonstrates	proposes
holds	recommends
illustrates	shows

Argues against
The verb indicates that the source is providing evidence against a position.

attacks	disputes
contradicts	objects
criticizes	opposes
denies	rebuts
differs	refutes
disagrees	

States controversially
The source makes a statement that you are skeptical about (be careful of your tone if you use these).

alleges
assumes
claims
purports

Implies
The source presents information either tentatively or indirectly.

implies
insinuates
proposes
suggests

Continues
You continue to refer to or quote the source.

adds
also notes
continues
goes on to say
states further

Concludes
The source draws a conclusion from previous discussion.

concludes
decides
determines
finds

Use a colon with introductory sentences

A particularly effective introduction is to include a sentence that presents helpful information to your reader about the nature or role of the quotation, followed by a colon. When your reader comes upon a quotation, an obvious question is, How does this quotation fit into and advance the central idea of the paper? Here are some examples that help answer that question:

♦ Doe prefers an alternative approach:
♦ Doe reported that the source of the problem lies in a lack of early data:
♦ Doe distinguishes between the two:
♦ Doe reminds us of the idea's origin:
♦ Doe provided a possible solution to this problem:

- ◆ Doe argues that the evidence supports the earlier theory:
- ◆ Doe is careful to qualify the claims made by the Midland group:
- ◆ In support of this interpretation, Doe cites the change in temperature:
- ◆ After 23 years of research, Doe is ready to report the findings:
- ◆ A recent study based on a sample of 63,000 users of the medication found that the side effects were varied but moderate:

Use an introductory phrase

Depending on the particular context of your source inclusion, you may want to use an introductory phrase rather than an introductory sentence. Here are some examples:

- ◆ In the words of Doe,
- ◆ According to John Doe,
- ◆ In Doe's view,
- ◆ As Doe tells us,
- ◆ As argued in the *American Journal of Ontological Epistemology,*
- ◆ In the survey analyst's judgment,
- ◆ As first reported by researchers in *Supercollider Monthly,*
- ◆ To quote the report directly,
- ◆ Quoting Doe again,

A QUICK TAKE ON CITATION

Examples throughout this book are presented in both APA and MLA citation styles. Here is a quick overview of basic in-text citation style.

APA

For APA quotations, include the author's last name, year, and page number (with a *p.*):

- • Jones (2009) discovered that "something is true" (p. 245).
- • Researchers recently found, "Something is true" (Smith, 2008, p. 321).
- • Several solutions were suggested in 2005 by Doe, including "the use of wax" (p. 432).

MLA

For MLA quotations, include the author's first and last name when mentioning them in the text, or the last name if in the citation, and the page number (without a *p.*):

- • John Smith agrees: "The preflight check was performed correctly" (123).
- • Jane Doe argues that "the word in line four should be *tattered,* not *tottered"* (456).
- • The forensics expert testified that "the luminol test revealed blood" (Jones 12).

When you use an introductory phrase, the quotation itself must be a complete sentence, or you must supply additional introductory words to make a complete sentence. The goal is to create a flowing, clear, contextualized discussion that the reader can follow easily. You are free to supply whatever introductory words best maintain the flow while remaining faithful to the source's meaning.

Example 4.2.1
Phrase introduction with quoted whole sentence, APA style:
According to Doe (2003), "The poet's personal letters were not discovered until 1915" (p. 567).

Phrase introduction with quoted whole sentence, MLA style:
According to Jane Doe, "The poet's personal letters were not discovered until 1915" (567).

Example 4.2.2
Phrase introduction with quoted partial sentence, APA style:
In Doe's analysis (2004), the market for suntan lotion was "not entirely seasonal, but largely seasonal" (p. 345).

Phrase introduction with quoted partial sentence, MLA style:
In Jane Doe's analysis, the market for suntan lotion is "not entirely seasonal, but largely seasonal" (345).

Comment:
Note that when you quote part of a sentence, you do not need to add leading ellipses because it is clear that the source is being quoted beginning in mid-sentence. See Section 4.4 for further information about punctuating quotations.

Use both set-off and built-in quotations

A set-off quotation is presented to the reader in a formal way, with an introductory phrase, verb, or sentence, followed by a comma or colon. The quotation itself begins with a capital letter and usually consists of a complete sentence.

Example 4.2.3
Set off with comma, APA style:
In a recent analysis of weather forecasting, Doe (2009) wrote, "The accuracy of forecasts has increased remarkably as new technologies have become available" (p. 432).

Set off with comma, MLA style:
In a recent analysis of weather forecasting, Jane Doe writes, "The accuracy of forecasts has increased remarkably as new technologies have become available" (432).

Example 4.2.4
Set off with colon, APA style:
Doe (2009) expressed caution about forecasts: "Never bet your umbrella on a forecast" (p. 234).

Set off with colon, MLA style:
John Doe is cautious about forecasts: "Never bet your umbrella on a forecast" (234).

A built-in quotation places the quotation into a subordinate clause beginning with *that* and attaches the clause to the writer's sentence. The built-in quotation can be an entire sentence from the source, an entire clause from a sentence, or just a partial sentence such as a long phrase. There is no comma or initial capital letter at the beginning of the quotation because the source's words are so closely built in to the paper writer's sentence. Instead of a formal division between writer's sentence and source's words, the built-in quotation flows seamlessly along as a part of the same sentence (clearly identified, of course, by quotation marks):

> **Example 4.2.5**
> Built-in whole clause with *that*, APA style:
> In a recent review of the history of weather forecasting, Doe (2009) wrote that "the accuracy of forecasts has increased remarkably as new technologies have become available" (p. 432).
>
> Built-in whole clause with *that*, MLA style:
> In a recent review of the history of weather forecasting, Jane Doe writes that "the accuracy of forecasts has increased remarkably as new technologies have become available" (432).
>
> **Example 4.2.6**
> Built-in partial sentence with *that*, APA style:
> In a recent look at the history of weather forecasting, Doe (2009) noted that the reliability of forecasts "has increased remarkably as new technologies have become available" (p. 432).
>
> Built-in partial sentence with *that*, MLA style:
> In a recent look at the history of weather forecasting, Jane Doe notes that the reliability of forecasts "has increased remarkably as new technologies have become available" (432).

Use the historical present tense for MLA-style papers

Students sometimes ask, "Because all of our sources were written in the past (even last week is now the past), shouldn't we be writing, 'John Doe *said*' instead of 'John Doe *says*'?" Other students ask a related question: "I can understand using *says* for a writer who is still alive, but what about a writer who has been dead for hundreds of years?"

The historical present tense is a convention in the humanities (English, history, and philosophy, for example) that discusses and quotes all sources in the present tense. The historical present has the conceptual benefit of treating all ideas as equally alive and active, "in play," and available for consideration. As a practical benefit, the historical present helps your own writing to be more lively and interesting because you seem to be describing something happening right now rather than in the past.

Good advice, then, is to use the historical present tense for your papers where all of the ideas are still under active consideration. (This practice will also prevent your papers from falling into random tense shifting—changing back and forth unthinkingly between past and present tense—a common ailment in research-paper writing.) If you are comparing changes between the past and present or referring to ideas no longer active, it is acceptable to use the past tense. See Example 4.3.5 below.

For APA-style papers, the present tense is restricted, but still used when discussing conclusions and current beliefs, as mentioned earlier.

4.3 Quoting strategies

Quoting a complete sentence or two is certainly a common and usually effective way of bringing a writer's words into your paper. But it is only one way, and there are other ways that can be more effective, depending on the particular circumstances. Using different strategies for the sake of variety and interest is by itself a good reason to have several choices. Another reason is that just the right strategy at the right time can give your writing added power and emphasis. This section offers more ideas for incorporating quotations into your writing.

Interrupt quotations

When you quote a complete sentence using a set-off introduction, you can do so according to Examples 4.2.3 and 4.2.4 above, or you can divide the quotation into two pieces for the purpose of variety or emphasis. The pause in the middle of the quotation and then resuming add an energy and emphasis that would not be present if you delivered the entire quotation at once. Because the position of most emphasis in a sentence is at the end, you create two emphases by artificially producing two ends. In the following example, note how "increased remarkably" gains more emphasis and attention than if the sentence were quoted whole.

Example 4.3.1
Divided quotation, APA style:
In a recent analysis, Doe (2009) noted the advances in the weather business. "The accuracy of forecasts has increased remarkably," she writes, "as new technologies have become available" (p. 432).

Divided quotation, MLA style:
In a recent analysis, Jane Doe notes the advances in the weather business. "The accuracy of forecasts has increased remarkably," she writes, "as new technologies have become available" (432).

Comment:
Note that the second piece of the sentence is a continuation of the first part, so that no capital letter is used and commas are appropriate. If you quote two separate sentences in this divided fashion, however, you will need a period ending the first sentence and a capital letter beginning the new, independent sentence. Otherwise, you will have a comma splice. Below is an example of two sentences with an intervening comment.

Example 4.3.2
Two sentences, divided by comment, APA style:
Doe (2009) reminded us that a recalled product is often not sent anywhere: "The order means that an identified fault must be remedied by the manufacturer." In actual practice, she added, "The remedy often involves only the mailing of new parts to the consumer or a visit to a repair center" (p. 456).

Two sentences, divided by comment, MLA style:
Jane Doe reminds us that a recalled product is often not sent anywhere: "The order means that an identified fault must be remedied by the manufacturer." In actual practice, she adds, "The remedy often involves only the mailing of new parts to the consumer or a visit to a repair center" (456).

Leave out some words

An effective method of reducing a source's words while retaining the benefit of quoting exact words (rather than summarizing) is to leave out the words of lesser importance. (See Section 4.4 for information about using ellipsis dots to show that words have been omitted from a quoted source.)

Remember that when you omit words from anywhere in the sentence, and especially in the middle, you must be sure that the sentence still makes grammatical sense, and that you have not introduced an error such as a sentence fragment or comma splice.

Also, be sure that omitting the words does not change the meaning of the sentence so that it no longer reflects the writer's actual view. Recall the discussion of the fallacy of vicious abstraction earlier in this chapter. Always do a meaning check after you delete some words, and make sure the overall meaning of the sentence has not changed.

That said, note how effective it can be to use just some of the source's words:

Example 4.3.3
Source:
Since its invention, the trend in video camera manufacture, like that of virtually all technology, has been toward the smaller, until we now have a camera that can be swallowed. —John Doe, 2008, p. 132

Beginning omitted, APA style:
As Doe (2008) stated, the development of the video camera "has been toward the smaller, until we now have a camera that can be swallowed" (p. 132).

Beginning omitted, MLA style:
As John Doe states, the development of the video camera "has been toward the smaller, until we now have a camera that can be swallowed" (132).

Middle omitted, APA style:
Technology researcher Doe (2008) indicated the direction of video design: "Since its invention, the trend in video camera manufacture . . . has been toward the smaller, until we now have a camera that can be swallowed" (p. 132).

Middle omitted, MLA style:
Technology researcher John Doe indicates the direction of video design: "Since its invention, the trend in video camera manufacture . . . has been toward the smaller, until we now have a camera that can be swallowed" (132).

End omitted, APA style:
Doe (2008) reported on this trend toward miniaturization: "Since its invention, the trend in video camera manufacture, like that of virtually all technology, has been toward the smaller . . ." (p. 132).

End omitted, MLA style:
John Doe reports on this trend toward miniaturization: "Since its invention, the direction in video camera manufacture, like that of virtually all technology, has been toward the smaller . . ." (132).

Quote phrases

Often, the most powerful quoting can be accomplished by using short phrases rather than entire sentences. By selecting just the phrase or phrases that best capture the idea you want to emphasize, you can build them into an appropriate sentence. Quoted phrases call attention to themselves because of their brevity and the highlighting effect produced by the quotation marks.

Example 4.3.4
Web article, no author, APA style:
The Tapwater Beverage Company promised that its new bottled water product would be manufactured using "state-of-the-art reverse osmosis filtration" that would guarantee "superiority of both purity and taste" ("Tapwater Enters," 2008).

Web article, no author, MLA style:
The Tapwater Beverage Company promises that its new bottled water product will be manufactured using "state-of-the-art reverse osmosis filtration" that will guarantee "superiority of both purity and taste" ("Tapwater Enters").

Comment:
In the example above, the name of the company that owns the Web site is used as the opening boundary marker and a shortened version of the title of the article is used for the close. On the References page (for APA) or Works Cited page (for MLA), the article would be listed alphabetically by the first word of the title, and the entire title would be spelled out: "Tapwater Enters Bottled Water Business."

Using only the phrases that best contain the meaning of the sentence also allows you not only to omit extraneous material but also to adapt a sentence's tense, point of view, and other elements to produce agreement with your own writing. The following example clarifies this:

Example 4.3.5
Source:
We have no plans to expand into Asian markets at this time. —Jane Doe, 2005, p. 234

Tense and point-of-view change made, APA style:
In 2005, Doe announced that the company had "no plans to expand into Asian markets" at the time (p. 234). However, within a year, it was building distribution warehouses in three Asian countries.

Tense and point-of-view change made, MLA style:
In 2005, Jane Doe announced that the company had "no plans to expand into Asian markets" at the time (234). However, within a year, it was building distribution warehouses in three Asian countries.

Comment:
The source is an announcement made in the present tense, while the writer wants to use the past tense to recount past events. The announcement was also made in the first person plural (*we*) while the user of the source wants to use third person singular (*the company* and *it*). These changes are made outside the quotation. Then the quoted words are built into the sentence with the desired revisions.

Important note: Remember that when you put words within quotation marks, you are promising your reader that those are the source's exact words. The rule for quotation, then, is this:

> **Always quote exactly.**

If words need to be changed, change words outside the quotation marks and quote only exact words. Use ellipsis dots to delete words within a quotation and square brackets to insert any words you are adding to make the meaning of the quotation clear. Never silently alter any quoted words. See Section 4.4 for information and examples relating to the use of ellipsis dots and square brackets.

4.4 Punctuating quotations

Minding your periods and commas in the papers you write is important not only because accuracy is important for scholarliness—and a good grade—but because readers take their cues from the quality (the accuracy and consistency) of your presentation to help them decide how reliable your ideas are. So, when it comes to punctuation, take it seriously. The byword is scrupulous meticulousness.

General conventions

When you use a source that follows British rather than American conventions for quotation (such as using single rather than double quotation marks), you should convert the punctuation use to American conventions while leaving the spelling and grammar of the original unchanged. The reason for this is that punctuation is traditionally considered a printer's convention, and every document should be consistent in its conventions.

Here is a summary of the most common American conventions for punctuating quotations.

QUOTATION RULE	EXAMPLE
1. Quotations use double quotation marks.	"Follow American conventions," he says.
2. Periods and commas go inside quotation marks.	The instructor says, "Remember where the comma goes," and adds, "and periods, too."
3. Quoting within a quotation uses single quotation marks.	The waiter said, "Our cake has been called 'chocolate decadence' by the food critics."
4. Quoting one word uses double quotation marks. The punctuation goes inside.	She called the spa "rejuvenating" and "fun."
5. A parenthetical citation is part of the sentence but not part of the quotation.	APA: The book says, "Try this" (p. 123). MLA: The book says, "Try this" (123).

Rule 2 above is perhaps the most commonly broken in student writing. Unless you have a citation that moves the period after the parentheses (see Rule 5), periods and commas go inside the quotation mark.

Rule 4 emphasizes quoting a single word as a quotation from a source. Be sparing in your use of quotation marks to call attention to your use of a word, with the implication that you disagree with the appropriateness of the use. Such a practice is known as using *scare quotes* or *sneer quotes* because the quoter seems to be sneering at the source's use of the words. Further, take care to avoid putting any of your own words in sneer quotes, as if you disavow the words themselves. As you can see, such a "habit" is usually seen as a sign of "immaturity," and is not an "effective" writing "practice."

Research papers that mix conventions (sometimes putting commas inside quotation marks, sometimes outside, for example) appear to be careless and unprofessional, as if the writer had not performed even basic proofreading. Consistency is necessary for—and at least implies—accuracy (though, of course, it might not involve accuracy), while inconsistency broadcasts inaccuracy and sends an unflattering message to the reader about the writer's competence.

Ellipsis

Words cannot be omitted or added to a quotation unless you inform your reader that you are altering the quotation from its original form. To do this, use ellipsis dots (or ellipses, plural of ellipsis) to show where you have omitted words, and use brackets to show where you have inserted words.

Ellipsis dots consist of three periods with spaces between them. They are used to indicate the omission of words from the middle or at the end of a quotation (but not the beginning). With publication of the most recent versions of the *Publication Manual of the American Psychological Association* (6th ed., APA, 2010) and the *MLA Handbook for Writers of Research Papers* (7th ed., MLA, 2009) ellipsis dots follow the same conventions.

> **Example 4.4.1**
> Source:
> Do not tie your shoe in a melon patch or adjust your hat under a pear tree.
> —Chinese Proverb
>
> Ellipsis in the middle of the sentence:
> APA Style:
> A Chinese proverb reminds us to avoid actions that casual observers may misinterpret: "Do not . . . adjust your hat under a pear tree."
>
> MLA Style:
> A Chinese proverb reminds us to avoid actions that casual observers may misinterpret: "Do not . . . adjust your hat under a pear tree."
>
> Comment:
> Words omitted from the middle of the quotation are indicated by three spaced periods.
>
> Ellipsis dots and a period at the end of a sentence:
> APA Style:
> The Chinese proverb says, "Do not tie your shoe in a melon patch. . . ."

MLA Style:
The Chinese proverb says, "Do not tie your shoe in a melon patch. . . ."

Comment:
When the ellipsis is at the end of the sentence, there is a fourth dot, which is the period ending the sentence. The period follows the last letter.

Ellipsis dots and a period at the end, but with intervening parenthetical material:
APA Style:
We should be careful to avoid suspicious behavior: "Do not tie your shoe in a melon patch . . ." (Chinese proverb).

MLA Style:
We should be careful to avoid suspicious behavior: "Do not tie your shoe in a melon patch . . ." (Chinese proverb).

Comment:
If there is a citation at the end, the period moves from after the last letter of the quotation to after the end of the citation.

Ellipsis dots are not used to show initial words omitted:
APA Style:
A Chinese proverb says not to "tie your shoe in a melon patch. . . ."

MLA Style:
A Chinese proverb says not to "tie your shoe in a melon patch. . . ."

Comment:
The omission of words from the beginning of a quotation does not need to be signaled because the quotation is clearly beginning mid-sentence or begins with a lower-case letter. The omission at the end needs to be indicated to let the reader know that more words follow in the original source.

Square brackets

Square brackets are used to add words inside a quotation. Parentheses are not used because they would indicate that the author of the source was making a parenthetical comment, and confusion would result. Note the difference:

Example 4.4.2
Incorrect use of parentheses inside a quotation, APA style:
Harris (2011) wrote, "Square brackets (also called, simply, brackets) are used to add words inside a quotation" (p. 56).

Correct use of square brackets inside a quotation, APA style:
Harris (2011) wrote, "Square brackets [also called, simply, brackets] are used to add words inside a quotation" (p. 56).

In the first situation, your reader will likely think that I (the author) added the words "also called, simply, brackets" as a parenthetical aside, which is incorrect. In the second example, using square brackets makes it clear that you, quoting me, added the additional words.

Inserting one or more words may be desirable under several circumstances.

- **To clarify a pronoun by adding the word to which it refers.** This word, the antecedent, may be in a previous sentence not included in the quotation. See Example 4.4.3.
- **To add clarity or explanation.** Quoting part of an author's work means, by definition, that you are losing some of the context of the quotation. Thus, it is sometimes necessary to supply a few words to clarify what the source is referring to by a specific term, reference, allusion, or other comment. See Example 4.4.4.
- **To expand an acronym.** Some sources reflect the acronym-laden specialty about which they are writing. They assume that their reader knows the meaning. However, your reader might not, so be sure to present the words behind the acronym the first time it occurs, whether in your own writing or in a quotation. See Example 4.4.5.
- **To identify an obvious error in the source text,** so that it will not appear to be a copying mistake. The Latin word *sic* (meaning *thus*) is used. The word is italicized in APA style but not in MLA style. And note that, whatever the nature of the error, you should not add an exclamation point after the *sic*, as if you are astonished that such an error could be made. See Example 4.4.6.

Example 4.4.3
Source:
A question arose about the impact of the wheel rim on the road at the time of the accident. Examination revealed that fresh gouges were clearly visible where it contacted the pavement. —Joseph Doe, 2007, p. 623

Example of adding an antecedent, APA style:
The forensic investigation "revealed that fresh gouges were clearly visible where it [the rim of the wheel] contacted the pavement" (Doe, 2007, p. 623).

Example of adding an antecedent, MLA style:
The forensic investigation "revealed that fresh gouges were clearly visible where it [the rim of the wheel] contacted the pavement" (Doe 623).

Comment:
Whenever the antecedent for a pronoun (it, him, her, they, we) is not present, clarify it either in the introduction to the quotation or within the quotation in square brackets.

Example 4.4.4
Source:
Hikers made the trek to both mountain and desert weather stations and retrieved the recording drum data. The sampling records were examined for levels of the same atmospheric gasses. —Jane Smith, 2008, p. 654

Example of adding a clarifying explanation, APA style:
Smith (2008) discovered that the investigation included data from both high and low altitude: "The sampling records [from weather stations in the desert and the mountains] were examined for levels of the same atmospheric gasses" (p. 654).

Example of adding a clarifying explanation, MLA style:
Jane Smith notes that the investigation included data from both high and low altitude: "The sampling records [from weather stations in the desert and the mountains] were examined for levels of the same atmospheric gasses" (654).

Comment:
An alternative to adding the clarification in square brackets inside the quotation is to add it to the introductory lead in or to the sentence following the quotation. Thus, for this example, the writer might have either introduced the quotation or added a follow-up sentence like this: "Jane Smith notes that the investigation included data from both mountain and desert weather stations."

Example 4.4.5
Source:
In many call centers, there is a constant tension between helping the customer and meeting AHT goals. —John Doe, 2008, p. 765

Example of expanding the acronym, APA style:
As Doe (2008) noted, "In many call centers, there is a constant tension between helping the customer and meeting AHT [Average Handle Time] goals"(p. 765).

Example of expanding the acronym, MLA style:
"In many call centers," writes John Doe, "there is a constant tension between helping the customer and meeting AHT [Average Handle Time] goals" (765).

Example 4.4.6
Source:
The general's words, however, should be understood in the context of the surrounding battle. —Brown, 2004, p. 123

Example of inserting *sic*, APA style:
One historian said that General Smervitz has been misunderstood: "The general's words, however, should be understood in the conrext [*sic*] of the surrounding battle" (Brown, 2004, p. 123).

Example of inserting *sic*, MLA style:
One historian says that General Smervitz has been misunderstood: "The general's words, however, should be understood in the context [sic] of the surrounding battle" (Brown 123).

Important: Note that when you add bracketed words to a sentence, you may not silently remove any of the words of the text. In Example 4.4.3 above, for instance, when supplying the antecedent to *it*, the *it* must remain. If you remove a word or words, then you must show that text is missing by including ellipsis dots in the appropriate place.

Review questions

To see how well you understand this chapter, attempt to answer each of the following questions without referring to the text. (Write down your answers to make checking easier.) Then check your answers with the text. If you missed something important, add it to your answer.

1. What are the reasons for choosing to quote rather than to paraphrase?

2. Describe the ways quotations can be used unwisely.

3. Define the fallacy of vicious abstraction and give an example.

4. List as many different introductory verbs as you can in one minute. Next, explain why having a choice of these words can improve your writing.

5. What is historical present tense, and why is it used?

6. Why is it important to pay attention to the accuracy of your punctuation?

Questions for thought and discussion

Use these questions for in-class or small-group discussion, or for stimulating your own thinking.

1. Write ten introductory lead-ins, making each one different (see pages 44–45 for examples). Which are your favorites, and why?

2. Which quoting strategies discussed in this chapter appeal to you most?

3. What strategies or techniques did you learn from this chapter that you plan to use in your research paper writing?

4. Have you ever intentionally padded a paper with long quotations or with many quotations? If so, why?

5. Has anyone ever quoted you out of context so that your words were misunderstood? If so, how did you feel? What did you do? Explain.

Name _____   Course _____

Chapter 4 Review: True-false quiz

Directions: In each case, determine whether the statement is true or false.

1. It is *not* a good idea to quote a source whose style and vocabulary are different from modern American usage.
   ☐ True   ☐ False

2. If a source makes a highly controversial claim or uses inflammatory language, quoting the source rather than paraphrasing it will help distance you from responsibility for the idea.
   ☐ True   ☐ False

3. Generally speaking, the more quotations you have in your paper, the better, because that will show how thorough your research has been.
   ☐ True   ☐ False

4. Leaving words out of a source's sentence in a way that changes the meaning commits the fallacy of vicious abstraction even if you use ellipsis dots.
   ☐ True   ☐ False

5. The fallacy of vicious abstraction can occur when a writer mistakenly believes that a source is advocating an idea that the source is merely describing.
   ☐ True   ☐ False

6. A well-chosen introductory verb before a quotation can give your reader information about the purpose or intended effect of the quotation.
   ☐ True   ☐ False

7. When quoting a source from more than five years ago, you should use past-tense verbs, such as *said*, rather than present-tense verbs such as *says*.
   ☐ True   ☐ False

8. You should always quote complete sentences to offset the source's words from your own writing.
   ☐ True   ☐ False

9. It is permissible to make an unnoted change in a word or two in a source's sentence in order to make a quotation fit your sentence better grammatically.
   ☐ True   ☐ False

10. In American typographical convention, commas and periods go inside the quotation mark when the two marks appear next to the quotation mark.
    ☐ True   ☐ False

5
Paraphrasing and Summarizing

Look to the essence of a thing, whether it be a point
of doctrine, of practice, or of interpretation.
—Marcus Aurelius

The previous chapter showed you how to quote from your sources effectively. This chapter shows you two alternative methods of presenting source material: paraphrasing and summarizing. These two skills have their own techniques and requirements, which, learned well, will give you a full range of choices for incorporating source material.

♦ Learning how to paraphrase and summarize effectively will strengthen your writing substantially.

♦ Knowing when to choose among quoting, paraphrasing, and summarizing will help you prepare each source for optimal impact.

♦ Practicing proper paraphrasing and summarizing will help you avoid plagiarism.

5.1 Paraphrasing

Quoting is only one way to incorporate a source's ideas into your research paper. Another way is to paraphrase the source.

What is a paraphrase?

A paraphrase is a restatement or rewriting of a source in order to present the source's idea or meaning without actually quoting the source's words. That is to say:

> **A paraphrase converts a source's words**
> **into about the same number of your own words.**

Example 5.1.1
Source:
The emergency room medical intervention provided to the subject was deemed suboptimal to best practices by legal counsel, so the facility and the on-shift physician received a legal service declaring a therapeutic misadventure. —John Doe, 2005, p. 321

Example paraphrase, APA style:
Doe (2005) reported that, after the accident, attorneys for the patient decided that the treatment given in the emergency room was substandard in comparison with that of other hospitals, so they filed a malpractice lawsuit against the doctor on duty and the hospital (p. 321).

Example paraphrase, MLA style:
John Doe reports that, after the accident, attorneys for the patient decided that the treatment given in the emergency room was substandard in comparison with that of other hospitals, so they filed a malpractice lawsuit against the doctor on duty and the hospital (321).

Comment:
In this example, you can see that the paraphrase requires the same number of words as the source, and it includes all the ideas in the source, but the paraphrase is clearer and easier to understand.

Why and when to paraphrase

Any one of several conditions can make paraphrasing a good choice as a means of incorporating a source into your paper:

- ◆ **Arrangement for emphasis.** The rearrangement of ideas and sentence structure associated with the process of paraphrasing allows you to emphasize the ideas of importance to your paper. The end of a sentence or passage has the most emphasis, the beginning the second most, and the middle the least. Therefore, if your source mentions an important idea in the middle of a long sentence, your paraphrase can position the idea at the end for more impact.

- ◆ **Simplifying the material.** The material may need to be simplified either in sentence structure, vocabulary, or presentation. The source may be highly technical or specific to a particular discipline, while you may be writing for a more general audience. The complexity of the argument may make it difficult to follow. In such cases, you can simplify the material through a paraphrase. The act of paraphrasing will increase your own understanding of the source material, and the paraphrase itself will increase your reader's understanding.

- ◆ **Clarifying the meaning.** The material can be presented more clearly because the source has a difficult style or technical vocabulary. Some brilliant thinkers write poorly. Others encumber their writing with an excess of jargon, over use the passive voice, or otherwise render their words less effective than their ideas. Paraphrasing under these circumstances is useful. Quoting a source your reader cannot understand will not help your paper, but providing a clear paraphrase will.

- ◆ **Normalizing your paper's style.** While your paper might include sources from the highly sophisticated to the simple, you might want to maintain a uniform writing style. Further, the comprehension level of the paper should be kept consistent to match your audience. In such a case, paraphrasing sources allows you to convert them into your own style and vocabulary.

- ◆ **Keeping the same length.** If the length of the source does not need to be shortened (as a summary would do), or more details are desired than a summary would provide, a paraphrase is the right choice.

Example 5.1.2
Source:
The often-discussed Theory X, Theory Y, and Theory Z management styles, which are in essence varying descriptors of a philosophy of human motivation, have been in the atmosphere of leadership since the 1960s. —Jane Smith, 2007, pp. 345–346

Example paraphrase, APA Style:
In an article in *Management Review*, Smith (2007) observed that thinking about leadership has, since the 1960s, included those frequently talked about Theory X, Theory Y, and Theory Z approaches to managing, and she noted that these are actually different beliefs about employee motivation (pp. 345-346).

Example paraphrase, MLA Style:
In an article in *Management Review*, Jane Smith observes that thinking about leadership has, since the 1960s, included those frequently talked about Theory X, Theory Y, and Theory Z approaches to managing, and she notes that these are actually different beliefs about employee motivation (345-46).

Comment:
In her article, Jane Smith buried in mid-sentence what the research paper writer thought was her most important idea, that these management theories are about employee motivation. In the paraphrase, then, this thought was put at the end, to give it emphasis.

Paraphrasing ground rules

Because paraphrasing involves changing the source's words and the sequence of the source's ideas, you must take care not to produce a distorted result. In order to create a paraphrase that is ethical and appropriate, then, keep these guidelines in mind as you develop your skill in paraphrasing:

- ♦ **Use the same number of words.** Keep the paraphrase about the same number of words as the original, not omitting any significant features of the source material. Include each point, major and minor, from the original.
- ♦ **Preserve the meaning.** Take care to preserve the author's original meaning and to avoid taking the ideas out of context. What the author stressed as the main points of the passage should be kept as the main points of the paraphrase. The author's conclusions, point of view, and even attitude should be preserved.

Again, when you work on paraphrasing, take care that the result is a complete paraphrase, not a partial one that includes unquoted phrases from the source. Including strings of the source's words without using quotation marks is plagiarism. In order to avoid plagiarism, follow these guidelines for a successful paraphrase:

- ♦ **The paraphrase must be almost entirely in your own words:** new vocabulary (such as synonyms) and new phrases. Do not mix your own words with any of the source's words (unless you quote the source's words). (Of course, you may use the same technical terms, such as *chronic insomnia*, and the same helper words, such as *a, and, the, of, in, is*, and so forth.)
- ♦ **Use a different sentence structure from that of the source.** Recast the ideas into your own presentation. Do not copy the arrangement of clauses or other rhetorical structures.
- ♦ **In most cases, rearrange the order of the ideas.** You must include all of the points and ideas of the source, but you should rearrange them. For passages that require a specific sequence, such as scientific processes, historical events, or cause-and-effect descriptions, maintain the order of the source at the major steps. You still may wish to rearrange the discussion within each step.

♦ **Put quotation marks around any exact words you retain** from the source. Quoting particularly effective phrases from the source is not technically part of a paraphrase, but doing so can lend flavor and sparkle to the paraphrase. Just be sure to include quotation marks around each phrase you quote.

♦ **Provide a citation** that clearly gives credit to the source for the ideas in the paraphrase.

How to paraphrase

Now that we have discussed the theory and rationale for paraphrasing, and mentioned what to be aware of while creating paraphrases, let's look at the practical side. To create an effective paraphrase, follow these steps:

♦ **Read the source passage several times.** In order to get a complete understanding of the passage, read it over more than once. Consult a dictionary, if necessary, to define any words you do not know. Use your reading comprehension skills here: Read the passage, look away, think about what you just read, recite out loud what you think the passage means, and then check your understanding by looking at the passage again. This first step is crucial, for you cannot paraphrase a passage accurately if you do not understand it.

♦ **Outline the passage.** Use your own words and phrases for writing the outline so that you can be free to use them as the building blocks of your paraphrase. You might write the first version of the outline without consulting the passage, in order to avoid the temptation of borrowing words or phrases from it. Then, consult the passage again to ensure that the outline is accurate and complete. Remember that a paraphrase does not omit any ideas.

♦ **Rearrange the outline.** Change the order of items to reflect the order of emphasis you want to present in your paraphrase or to create better clarity. For example, the author may present a conclusion at the beginning of the passage, while you may want to put it at the end of your paraphrase.

♦ **Write the paraphrase.** Use the outline or your memory to write the paraphrase. Do not look at the source text. It is a good idea to write the paraphrase in several different ways, comparing the clarity, emphasis, and fidelity of each version to the source. Two or three variants will give you a choice later on when you want to build the source into your paper.

♦ **Check the result.** Compare the paraphrase with the original to be sure that you have preserved the source's meaning accurately. Be sure you have not accidentally included exact words or phrases you remembered from reading the source. (The technical term for this is *cryptomnesia*, inadvertently forgetting where you read phrases and thinking that they are your own.)

♦ **Add the appropriate citation.** A good idea is to include a possible lead-in as well, so that your paraphrase is appropriately introduced. Be sure the source is properly credited, using the citation style you have chosen or been assigned.

When you are finished, double-check the ground rules above to be sure they have been satisfied.

To help you understand the process better, study the following examples. In each case, follow the steps in the process and then compare the result with the source.

Example 5.1.3
Source text:
Invention, strictly speaking, is little more than a new combination of those images which have been previously gathered and deposited in the memory: nothing can come of nothing: he who has laid up no materials, can produce no combinations. —Sir Joshua Reynolds, *Discourses on Art*, 1797/1965, pp. 15-16

Outline using your own words:
(1) Creativity combines ideas or visual impressions already remembered.
(2) Everything needs a source or original.
(3) Without ideas or images, there is no raw material to intermix.

Rearrange, revising freely:
(3) Without a stock of ideas, there is no raw material to intermix to get a new product.
(2) Everything needs a source.
(1) Creativity in painting [thus] is an act of combining visual impressions seen and remembered.

Write using APA style of citation:
Reynolds (1797/1965) argued that without a stock of ideas, the artist would have no raw material to intermix to get a new idea because every creation needs a source. Creativity in painting is therefore an act of combining visual impressions the artist has seen and remembered (pp. 15-16).

Write using MLA style of citation:
Sir Joshua Reynolds argues that without a stock of ideas, the artist will have no raw material to intermix to get a new idea because every creation needs a source. Creativity in painting is therefore an act of combining visual impressions the artist has seen and remembered (15-16).

Comment:
Note here that the original quotation contains 39 words, while the paraphrase has 42. The ideas are all included, while the language is clarified and the concept of creativity ("invention" in the original) is placed last for emphasis. The introductory lead-in and citation information do not count as part of the paraphrase.

Example 5.1.4
Source text:
Historically, the quality of a decision has corresponded directly with the quantity of information resources available for making the decision. However, today the explosive increase in the quantity of information has created a new reality, that when a certain point is reached, referred to as information overload, the amount of information is such that it reduces the quality of the decision because the information can no longer be effectively processed. Thus, the overabundance of information actually inhibits rather than enhances decision quality. —John Doe, 2005, p. 123

Outline using your own words:
(1) In the past (or until recently), a better decision came from a larger amount of information.
(2) But now the amount of information is increasing so much that it can make decisions worse.

(3) Called information overload when too much information cannot all be taken into account.

(4) So, too much information can hurt rather than improve a decision.

Rearrange, revising here and there:

(3) Information overload results when too much information cannot all be taken into account.

(1) In the past, the larger the amount of information, the better the decision would be.

(2) But now the amount of information is increasing so much that it can make decisions worse.

(4) So, too much information can hurt rather than improve a decision.

Write using APA style of citation:

As Doe (2005) discussed, information overload occurs when so much information is present that it cannot all be taken into account. In the past, the more information available for making a decision, the better the decision would be. Today, however, there is so much information available for making most decisions that a point can be reached where acquiring still more information can be harmful. An attempt to take too much information into account hurts rather than helps the resulting decision (p. 123).

Write using MLA style of citation:

As John Doe tells us, information overload occurs when so much information is present that it cannot all be taken into account. In the past, the more information available for making a decision, the better the decision would be. Today, however, there is so much information available for making most decisions that a point can be reached where acquiring still more information can be harmful. An attempt to take too much information into account hurts rather than helps the resulting decision (123).

Comment:

The source text has been rearranged to emphasize the concept of information overload and to simplify the vocabulary and sentence structure. Length is comparable, with the source being 82 words and the paraphrase 76 words.

Example 5.1.5

Source text:

Retailers may use discounted-price sales in order to clear excess inventories. However, if price discounting occurs too frequently, customers might come to expect such events regularly and therefore defer purchases in anticipation of upcoming off-price events. In such a case, this shifted buying pattern will reduce the retailer's full-margin volume and possibly only worsen the excess inventory problem. —Jane Doe, 2009, p. 321

Outline using your own words:

(1) Some stores have regular lower-price sales to reduce the oversupply of merchandise.

(2) If there are too many sales, customers will begin to take them for granted.

(3) Customers will then put off buying from the store until a sale is on.

(4) This behavior will lower the number of goods sold at full price.

(5) These lower sales may increase the oversupply of merchandise.

Rearrange:

(1) Some stores have regular lower-price sales to reduce the oversupply of merchandise.

(5) These lower sales may increase the oversupply of merchandise.

(3) Customers will then put off buying from the store until a sale is on.

(2) If there are too many sales, customers will begin to take them for granted.
(4) This behavior will lower the number of goods sold at full price.

Write using APA style citation:
Some stores, according to Doe (2009), employ regular lower-price sales in order to reduce the oversupply of merchandise on hand, but this practice can actually increase the oversupply. When sales occur too often, customers will wait for a sale before buying because they take the sale opportunities for granted. This behavior will lower the number of goods sold at full price, leaving them in inventory (p. 321).

Write using MLA style citation:
Some stores, according to Jane Doe, employ regular lower-price sales in order to reduce the oversupply of merchandise on hand, but this practice can actually increase the oversupply. When sales occur too often, customers will wait for a sale before buying because they take the sale opportunities for granted. This behavior will lower the number of goods sold at full price, leaving them in inventory (321).

Comment:
The source text has been rearranged to highlight the unintended effects of too-frequent sales on inventory. Sentences (2) and (3) have been intermixed in the paraphrase. As with the other examples above, note that the writer is free to improve, add, and delete words from the outline, even though the outline is written in complete sentences, paraphrasing each source sentence. Length of the two passages is comparable, with the source at 58 words and the paraphrase at 61.

Cautions about paraphrasing

Following the guidelines and the instructions discussed above should help you write effective paraphrases. However, you should still be on the alert to avoid the most common errors of paraphrasing:

- **Changing only some of the words.** Writers who change only a few words or who include various phrases from the source in the paraphrase commit plagiarism. As the instructions above note, all of the words must be different (other than technical terms under discussion, such as *information overload* and the helper words, such as *the, and, of,* etc.).
- **Changing words but keeping the same sentence structure and order of presentation.** Paraphrasing must be more than substituting synonyms for every word in the original. Rewrite the source.
- **Adding ideas or explanation.** The paraphrase should reflect the source accurately, and must not include ideas absent from the source. Explanation of the paraphrase should come in your own subsequent discussion, not in the paraphrase itself.
- **Adding interpretation or assessment.** The paraphrase should not include your evaluation or judgment of the ideas. Evaluate afterwards. Avoid also any biased presentation of the meaning, such as the use of emotive, belittling, or sarcastic words in the paraphrase. Rise above such unjust tactics.
- **Creating a straw man fallacy.** Writers who exaggerate or misrepresent the source in a way that makes it an easier target for rebuttal commit the straw man fallacy. Take care that your paraphrase is fair, especially if you are hos-

tile toward the source. See the example below (the version labeled "Straw man fallacy paraphrase").

Example 5.1.6
Source:
Unless steps are taken to provide a predictable and stable energy supply in the face of growing demand, the nation may be in danger of sudden power losses or even extended blackouts, thus damaging our industrial and information-based economies. Building more gas-fired generation plants seems to be the best answer. —John Doe, 2007, p. 231

Fair paraphrase, APA style:
Doe (2007) believes that we must construct additional power plants fueled by natural gas if we are to have a reliable electricity supply during this period of increasing usage. Without that, the country's economic base (both industrial and information-driven) may be damaged by lengthy blackouts or abrupt losses of power (p. 231).

Inadequate paraphrase, APA style:
Doe (2007) recommended that the government take action **to provide a predictable and stable energy supply** because of constantly **growing demand**. Otherwise, we may be in danger of losing power or even experiencing **extended blackouts**. These circumstances could **damage our industrial and information-based economy**. He says that **gas-fired plants** appear **to be the best answer** (p. 231).

Comment:
The writer of this inadequate paraphrase commits plagiarism by including many word-for-word phrases from the source (indicated by the bold type). The order of the ideas is also unchanged from the source. Changing only a few words in a source creates an inadequate paraphrase because it plagiarizes the remainder of the source.

Straw man fallacy paraphrase, APA style:
Doe (2007) claimed that if we do not litter the whole country with a bunch of heavily polluting power plants, there would be no way to ensure a reliable supply of power in the face of constantly growing wasteful usage. Without all those new plants, he alleged, our whole economy will collapse, and we will all be cast into permanent darkness (p. 231).

Comment:
The straw man fallacy paraphrase is not only a mischaracterization of Doe, attributing extremist claims to him ("economy will collapse," "permanent darkness"), but it also uses highly emotive terms to sneer at the writer and his argument ("claimed," "litter," "alleged"). Interpretations of the facts are also added to the paraphrase ("heavily polluting," "wasteful"). Remember that the place to attack a position you reject is *after* you have presented the author's position as accurately as you can.

5.2 Summarizing

In addition to quoting and paraphrasing, your third choice for incorporating a source into your own writing is to summarize it. Summarizing possesses a flexibility that allows for highly creative uses of source material. While there is no degree of paraphrasing (a paraphrase must contain about the same number of words as the source), a summary can be created with many fewer or only somewhat fewer words.

What is a summary?

A summary is a condensed restatement or rewriting of a source in order to present the source's idea in a more focused or shorter way than quoting or paraphrasing would allow. In other words:

> A summary reduces a source's words into fewer of your own words.

Example 5.2.1

Source:

Fromage swept the huge sand vacuum back and forth along an arc parallel to the boat, getting deeper and deeper in a fixed area. After a few minutes, he heard the thud of something more solid than sand hitting the walls of the vacuum. Then he looked down on the sea floor. Something glinted at him. It was a coin. Then there was another. And two more. Three. A bar of silver. Suddenly, a whole cornucopia of coins and bars, both in gold and silver, lay before him as the vacuum drew off the overlying sand. —John Doe, 2005, p. 198 [96 words]

Summary:

At the moment of discovery of the treasure, Doe (2005) describes how Fromage used a sand vacuum to uncover first a coin, then another, and finally the load of precious metal bars and coins (p. 198). [32 words]

Why and when to summarize

The power of summarizing comes from its flexibility. A summary can shorten a source text moderately or dramatically, depending on your application. You may want to reduce a section from a book or article to about a third or a fourth of its original length, or you may want to summarize an entire article or even a book in a paragraph. A summary at its most condensed might involve a sentence, a phrase, or even only a single word or two. For example, if you have just presented an argument for a position, quoting and citing a source or two, you might continue to bolster your case by referring briefly to other sources that also argue in favor of your position: "This view is also supported by Jones (2001), Smith (2004), and Doe (2007)." Here, you have summarized each of these three sources by stating that they are in agreement with your argument.

A summary is a good choice in several circumstances:

- ♦ **Simplify the source.** An argument or discussion that may take several pages in the source can be condensed, clarified, and simplified. Stating just the principal reasons or points gets the information to the reader without derailing your own argument.
- ♦ **Eliminate the extras.** Unneeded examples, digressions, or explanations can be omitted, keeping only the essential parts of the discussion or the main argument. References to other discussions in the same book or article, which would be irrelevant to your readers, can be eliminated.
- ♦ **Condense the source.** Fewer details are needed than a paraphrase would provide. A summary can be a more general statement of the overall meaning of the source. Too much of another source tends to create an elaborate digression rather than a seamless support to your own discussion.

♦ **Make a minor point.** A source might contribute to your argument in a minor way, or you wish to refer to it only briefly. For example (MLA style), "John Doe agrees with Smith, using many of the same arguments" (234).

In order to avoid plagiarism, follow these guidelines for a successful summary:

♦ **The summary must be almost entirely in your own words:** new vocabulary (such as synonyms) and new phrases. Do not mix your own words with any of the source's words (unless you quote the source's words). (Once again, you may use the same technical terms and helper words as when paraphrasing.)

♦ **Use a sentence structure different from that of the source.** Recast the ideas into your own presentation.

♦ **Rearrange the order of the ideas.** A summary will omit some ideas, but the remaining ones should be reordered as well. (If you are summarizing a passage describing a process or necessary sequence of events, you may maintain the order of the source.)

♦ **Use quotation marks** around any exact words you retain from the source.

♦ **Provide a citation** that clearly gives the source credit for the ideas.

In order to create a summary that is ethical and appropriate, take care to preserve the author's original meaning and to avoid taking the ideas out of context. See the "Paraphrasing ground rules" on pages 63–64 for more information—the same rules apply to summarizing.

How to summarize

To create an effective summary, follow these steps:

♦ **Read the source passage several times.** In order to get a complete understanding of the passage, read it over more than once. Consult a dictionary, if necessary, to define any word you do not know. Use your reading comprehension skills here: Read the passage, look away, think about what you just read, recite out loud what you think the passage means, and then check your understanding by looking at the passage again. This step is crucial because you cannot summarize a passage accurately if you do not understand it.

♦ **Decide how long a summary you need.** Depending on your purpose, you may need a paragraph, a few sentences, one sentence, or part of a sentence. Keeping the length goal in mind will guide you in the remaining steps.

♦ **Outline the passage.** Use your own words and phrases for writing the outline so that you can be free to use them as the building blocks of your summary. As you outline, include the main points, but omit the supporting material you do not need. Be careful not to alter the meaning. If the source is short enough, you might attempt to write the outline without consulting the source, in order to avoid the temptation of borrowing words or phrases from it. Then check to be sure that you have included all the main ideas.

♦ **Rearrange the outline.** Change the order of the outline to reflect the order of emphasis you want to present in the summary.

♦ **Write the summary.** Use the outline to guide you, and do not look at the source text.

- **Check the result.** Compare the summary with the original to be sure that you have accurately preserved the source's meaning. Be sure that you have not accidentally included exact words or phrases you remembered from reading the source, or if you have, be sure to put quotation marks around them.
- **Add the appropriate citation.** In addition to crediting the source properly, you might also want to include an appropriate lead-in to the summary. You might not use exactly that lead-in for the final paper, but it will provide a possibility.

Example 5.2.2

Source text, with sentence numbers added for reference:
(1) Fire is both a devastating and a renewing event in the life of the forest. (2) An unchecked forest fire can clear thousands of acres, burning to ashes every tree, bush, and vine, together with the plant material on the forest floor that supplies mulch for vegetation, protection and food for insects, and (along with roots) erosion control. (3) Small animals and insects are killed off by the fire and heat while larger animals that survive temporarily by fleeing may live only to starve later because their food supply has been eliminated. (4) Without the erosion control of the forest plants, the winter rains can wash precious topsoil away, clogging rivers and killing fish and leaving an even more barren landscape. (5) However, the same fire that has caused this destruction also has cleansed the forest of dead or diseased trees. (6) Harmful pests (such as pine beetles) are killed, too. (7) Some types of seeds require the heat of a fire in order to germinate; they now have the opportunity to begin new life. (8) Other small seedlings are now able to grow also, freed from the deep shade and competition of the previous vegetation. (9) Even the ashes can add their chemistry to the soil. —Jane Doe, 2007, p. 132 [198 words]

Decide the length:
This summary should be one-fourth of the original (therefore, about 50 words here).

Outline using your own words and omitting lesser details:
(1) Fire can harm and help a forest.
(2) Trees, shrubs, dead leaves, and pine needles—all are burned to powder.
(3) Smaller wildlife is killed.
(4) Loss of roots and mulch can cause mudslides.
(5) Unhealthy trees have been purged from the forest by the fire.
(6) Insect pests have also been eliminated.
(7) Seeds that require heat to sprout can grow.
(8) Plants that could not compete with large trees can thrive, also.
(9) Ashes help the soil.

Rearrange:
(2) Trees, shrubs, dead leaves, and pine needles—all are burned to powder.
(4) Loss of roots and mulch can cause mudslides.
(3) Smaller wildlife is killed.
(6) Insect pests have also been eliminated.
(5) Unhealthy trees have been purged from the forest by the fire.
(9) Ashes help the soil.
(7) Seeds that require heat to sprout can grow.
(8) Plants that could not compete with large trees can thrive, also.
(1) Fire can harm and help a forest.

First draft:

In describing the effects of a forest fire, Doe (2007) pointed out that everything—trees, shrubs, leaves on the ground—is burned to powder, eliminating roots and mulch that would prevent mudslides. Even smaller wildlife is killed. However, she also noted that insect pests are killed as well, together with unhealthy trees. Their ashes have become a soil amendment. Seeds that require heat to sprout can now grow, and plants that would never grow in the deep shade of the forest can now thrive. In Doe's view, then, fire can be both harmful and helpful to a forest (p. 132). [93 words]

Comment:

This draft has reduced the passage by only about 50 percent. You may need to work through several drafts to achieve your length goal, since it is difficult to hit a length target on the first try. Measuring your progress sets up a new goal. Here, the new goal is to reduce the first summary draft by half.

Second draft:

In describing the effects of a forest fire, Doe (2007) pointed out that everything is burned to powder, eliminating both trees and the mulch that would prevent mudslides. Even smaller wildlife is killed. However, she further noted that insect pests are killed, also, together with unhealthy trees, turning their ashes into a soil amendment. Seeds that require heat to sprout can now grow. In Doe's view, then, fire can be both harmful and helpful to a forest (p. 132). [72 words]

Comment:

This draft contains 72 words. At this point, you may decide that the summary is as condensed as you need it and adopt this version for your paper. If you still want the 50-word version, you can reduce the draft further. Your new goal is to reduce this draft by one-third.

Third draft using APA citation style:

In a forest fire, Doe (2007) pointed out, everything is destroyed: Trees and mulch turn to ashes, and smaller wildlife is killed. However, she noted that insect pests and unhealthy trees are also turned to a soil-amending ash, while heat-sprouted seeds can now thrive. In Doe's view, then, a forest fire can be both harmful and helpful (p. 132). [53 words]

Third draft using MLA citation style:

In a forest fire, Jane Doe points out, everything is destroyed: Trees and mulch turn to ashes, and smaller wildlife is killed. However, she notes that insect pests and unhealthy trees are also turned to a soil-amending ash, while heat-germinating seeds can now grow. In Doe's view, then, a forest fire can be both harmful and helpful (132). [53 words]

Comment:

This draft is 53 words, close to our goal. When you work on several drafts of a text, hammering it down to fewer and fewer words, not only will you come to know the text itself very well, but you will also gain insights into exactly what you see as the important or even essential parts of the text. In addition, you will develop your writing skills further, as you wrestle with sentence structures and phrasings in an effort to hone down the number of words to meet your requirements. Summarizing can be an exciting challenge.

An alternative technique for summarizing is to construct a sentence outline that contains about the same number of words as the projected summary. In the situation above, for example, the outline would be limited to about 50 words. Writing a summary of the desired length based on the outline then becomes simpler. The challenge in this case lies in trimming down the ideas into an appropriate-length outline. You may wish to experiment to see which of these techniques works better for you.

Example 5.2.3
Source text: The fire passage in Example 5.2.2.
Goal: 50 words.
Strategy: Nine sentences must be reduced to an average length of 5 to 6 words each.

Outline:
(1) In a forest, fire can harm and help. [8 words]
(2) Everything is burned. [3 words]
(3) Small animals are killed immediately; others die from hunger later. [10 words]
(4) Erosion leaves the hills barren. [5 words]
(5) Dead and diseased trees are removed. [6 words]
(6) Harmful insects are killed. [4 words]
(7) Some seeds need fire heat to germinate. [7 words]
(8) Small plants can now grow freely. [6 words]
(9) Ashes fertilize the soil. [4 words]
Total words in the outline: 53.

Rearrange:
(2) Everything is burned.
(4) Erosion leaves the hills barren.
(3) Small animals are killed immediately; others die from hunger later.
(6) Harmful insects are killed.
(5) Dead and diseased trees are removed.
(9) Ashes fertilize the soil.
(7) Some seeds need fire heat to germinate.
(8) Small plants can now grow freely.
(1) In a forest, fire can harm and help.

Initial comment:
Starting with 53 words and realizing that the sentences will need glue words (transitions and conjunctions), we realize that our goal of 50 words is a challenge. Let's see what we can do.

Summary, APA style:
In a forest fire, noted Doe (2007), everything is burned, causing erosion to leave the hills barren—after the small animals are killed immediately and larger ones die from hunger later on. However, harmful insects are also killed and dead and diseased trees are removed. Ashes fertilize the soil, while some seeds need fire heat to germinate. And small plants can now grow freely. So, a forest fire can both harm and help. [70 words]

Comment:
This summary is a bit more awkward than the earlier ones because it follows the wording of the outline sentences so closely, and it still misses the 50-word goal by a relatively large margin. Good advice is to focus on writing an effective and engaging (and faithful) summary. Do not force yourself to use the exact sentences or phrases in your outline.

Cautions about summarizing

The cautions that apply to paraphrasing also apply to summarizing:

- **Be careful to use your own words and sentence structure** to write the summary.
- **Avoid adding your own ideas to the summary.** Do not spell out assumptions or other unstated ideas.
- **Avoid adding interpretive comments to the summary.** Your comments and interpretation should follow the summary.
- **Be careful to summarize fairly** and avoid creating a straw man fallacy.

See the section, "Cautions about paraphrasing" on pages 67-68 for detailed information about these cautions. In addition to these, there are two cautions relevant only to summaries:

- **Avoid presenting a minor point in the source as a major point.** When you summarize and omit various details, be careful that a minor point does not appear to be the main point of the passage (or article or book). If necessary, you can indicate a minor point with language such as "covers briefly," "also mentions," "adds that," and so on.
- **Avoid presenting a major point in the source as a minor point.** Unless you are careful, the omission of details, explanations, and examples can sometimes make a point that was discussed at great length appear less important than other, more minor, points in your summary. If necessary, you can clarify the difference between major and minor points: "One of Doe's most significant points is — ."

Source limitations on summarizing

As a final comment on the art of summarizing, it should be pointed out that some sources are much easier to reduce substantially in a summary than others. The reason for this is that the prose of some writers is already fairly compact, while that of others is more expanded. Some writers practice an intense verbal economy, writing crisp, often short sentences and getting their points across briefly. Others employ a verbose style, either because they use an abundance of words to express each thought or because they explore the byways and detours of thought while they write. Thus, condensing the text of an already terse writer will be more of a challenge than working with a more expanded text.

It is important, then, to get a feel for the relative density of the text you want to summarize before you establish a goal for reducing it. If you have a lengthy passage of very compact writing, you might decide to quote or paraphrase several sections rather than to summarize the entire passage.

5.3 Deciding whether to quote, paraphrase, or summarize

Your decision about which form of source use to apply for a given reference depends on many factors, including how well the source writes, whether you want to use an entire argument or just the crucial phrase, and so on. Reasons to use quotations, paraphrases, and summaries have been presented above in their respective sections. For some additional help in deciding how to incorporate a source's idea in your paper, you can use the following decision grid. The grid operates on the basis of how the source expresses the idea you want to incorporate into your paper.

QUOTE, PARAPHRASE, OR SUMMARIZE DECISION GRID

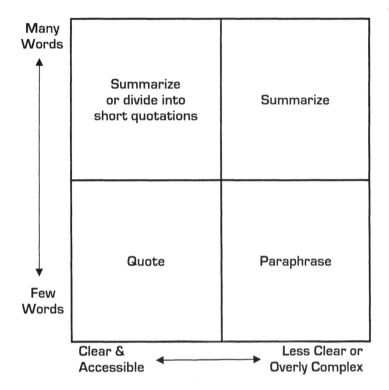

As you can see, there are four quadrants, and the decision is based on the interrelationship between (1) the number of words the source uses to present the information you want to use and (2) the degree of clarity and complexity of the source's presentation.

♦ If the information you want to use from the source is presented in just a few words that are clear and easily understood, then quotation is a likely choice.

♦ If the information is presented in few words, but the presentation is difficult to understand, then paraphrasing might be best.

♦ If the information requires many words but they are all clear and accessible (understandable), then you might either summarize or break the source up into several short quotations, discussing each one before quoting the next.

♦ If the information you need to include is in the form of both many words and complex or unclear words, then summarizing is a good choice.

5.4 Beware of thesaurusitis

The purpose of writing is to communicate, not to obscure your ideas by showing off an abstract vocabulary. A good vocabulary is important for the clearest expression, but choosing words merely for the sake of impressing the reader is a mistake. Words should be chosen for their accuracy and appropriateness to the context.

Thesaurusitis is a condition that often seizes young writers who wish to impress their readers. These writers use a thesaurus to look up many of the words they have written and then substitute the longest words they can find. Unknown to them, the result is not a seemingly sophisticated paper that impresses their instructor. Rather, the result is often quite comical, causing any educated reader to laugh at it. There are several reasons these thoughtless substitutions fail to be effective.

♦ **There are multiple levels of language use.** For example, a competent writer would not mix slang words with formal words like this: "Your honor, this bad dude has committed a serious violation of the traffic code." Similarly, some words are more fitting in a formal or an informal context. Except for slang or informal words, the thesaurus does not typically label which level of diction (language use) each word belongs to, and sometimes the usage practice is rather subtle. To put it another way, words cannot be mixed together without consideration of their usage level.

♦ **Synonyms often have only similar meanings.** The thesaurus contains synonyms, but a synonym often does not mean exactly the same thing as another word. More commonly, *a synonym means something similar to another word.* The similarity varies. You may have seen some of the comical results from using synonyms. Here is an example, constructed by using a synonym dictionary, showing that *love* means *hatred* because they are synonyms:

> Love is synonymous with Affection.
> Affection is synonymous with Concern.
> Concern is synonymous with Carefulness.
> Carefulness is synonymous with Exactness.
> Exactness is synonymous with Strictness.
> Strictness is synonymous with Criticism.
> Criticism is synonymous with Disapproval.
> Disapproval is synonymous with Aversion.
> Aversion is synonymous with Hatred.

♦ **Words are often used in ways that do not transfer to synonyms.** Figurative use of words and ideas, idioms, and even clichés affect the interpretation of words and phrases, changing their meaning from a literal understanding to something more nuanced. Suppose a student writes in a paper, "Last night my roommate was dead wrong about when the bookstore closed." Wanting to impress the instructor, the student looks up two words in the thesaurus and substitutes them this way: "Last night my roommate was deceased unlawful about when the bookstore closed." Clearly, *deceased* and *unlawful*, though synonyms for *dead* and *wrong*, respectively, cannot be thoughtlessly substituted for those words in just any situation. And yet, the resulting sentence is not much different from the writing many instructors receive.

Build your vocabulary as you read and study because the more words you know, the more exact you can be in your thinking and writing. Words should add clarity to ideas as you write, not muddy them. Do not use big words for their own sake; in other words (using the thesaurus), eschew the gratuitous utilization of sesquipedalian locutions. For the best writing, then, learn a lot of useful words and follow this advice:

> **When you write, use the words you know.**

Review questions

To see how well you understand this chapter, attempt to answer each of the following questions without referring to the text. (Write down your answers to make checking easier.) Then check your answers with the text. If you missed something important, add it to your answer.

1. What are some of the reasons to prefer paraphrasing a source?

2. Explain the difference between a paraphrase and a summary.

3. Define the straw man fallacy and give an example.

4. Describe the type of source material that would be better summarized than quoted or paraphrased.

5. When you paraphrase or summarize, what should you check to make sure the result is acceptable?

6. Define *thesaurusitis* and explain what makes it a problem rather than a benefit.

Questions for thought and discussion

Use these questions for in-class or small-group discussion, or for stimulating your own thinking.

1. When you write a paper, are you more likely to use one method of source use (quotation, paraphrase, or summary) over another? If so, why?

2. As you take notes, how do you make sure to identify the difference between a quotation and a summary or between a quotation and your own ideas? (In other words, what kind of note-taking system do you use?)

3. Now that you have read this chapter, do you feel more confident about choosing between quoting, paraphrasing, and summarizing? Explain.

4. Have you ever been quoted, paraphrased, or summarized in a newspaper, radio broadcast, or been in a discussion, only to find your words or ideas distorted or misrepresented? If so, how did you feel? What did you do? Explain.

Name _____   Course _____

Chapter 5 Review: True-false quiz

Directions: In each case, determine whether the statement is true or false.

1. If a source is written in a highly complex style, a paraphrase should maintain the complex style.
   ☐ True   ☐ False

2. When you paraphrase, you may repeat technical terms from the source.
   ☐ True   ☐ False

3. A paraphrase reduces the number of words needed to convey a source's ideas.
   ☐ True   ☐ False

4. You can use some of the source's words in a summary or paraphrase, but only if you put them in quotation marks.
   ☐ True   ☐ False

5. When you summarize, it is a good idea to indicate your attitude toward the source in the summary.
   ☐ True   ☐ False

6. A summary can be as short as a phrase or a sentence.
   ☐ True   ☐ False

7. Unneeded examples and digressions can be omitted from a summary of a source.
   ☐ True   ☐ False

8. A paraphrase should reflect the source's attitude toward the subject, rather than the paraphraser's attitude.
   ☐ True   ☐ False

9. A good way to paraphrase is to use the thesaurus in your word processor to replace the words in your source's sentences with synonyms.
   ☐ True   ☐ False

10. The straw man fallacy can occur when a writer paraphrases or summarizes a source in a way that inaccurately makes the source's ideas appear simplistic or ridiculous.
    ☐ True   ☐ False

11. The easiest way to paraphrase is just to take out some of the source's words, such as unneeded phrases and details. What's left will be an acceptable paraphrase.
    ☐ True   ☐ False

Name _____ Course _____

Chapter 5 Review: Acceptable use or plagiarism?

Directions: Read the source text and then compare it with each of the potential uses that follow. The potential uses may involve a summary, a paraphrase, or a combination, and may include quotation. In each case ask, "Is the potential use acceptable or does it commit plagiarism?" Explain your answers. (Note: This review uses APA citation style.)

Source text

If there is no approved treatment for an illness or condition, some people in the study may be given a placebo, while others get the new treatment being tested. The main reason to have a placebo group is to be sure that any effects that happen are actually caused by the treatment and not some other factor. The placebo looks, tastes, or feels just like the actual treatment, so that the patient's expectations alone are not responsible for the outcome. (American Cancer Society, 2009, How are placebos used? section, ¶3)

Potential use 1

When there is no treatment approved for an illness, some people may be given a placebo, while others will get the medicine being tested. The reason to give some in the group a placebo is to be sure that the results are actually caused by the medicine and not by some other factor. The placebo looks, tastes, and feels just like the real medicine, so that patient expectations are not responsible for the outcome. (American Cancer Society, 2009, How are placebos used? section, ¶3)

  ☐ Acceptable use   ☐ Plagiarism

Potential use 2

In the absence of an approved treatment for an illness or condition, a placebo is sometimes given to some people in the study, while others get the test medicine. Those people on placebos serve to ensure that any effects that happen are actually caused by the treatment. Placebos are designed to look, taste, and feel just like the real thing, preventing the patient's expectations from affecting the outcome of the study. (American Cancer Society, 2009, How are placebos used? section, ¶3)

  ☐ Acceptable use   ☐ Plagiarism

Potential use 3

According to the American Cancer Society (2009), when the effects of a new medicine or therapy are under investigation, a placebo group will sometimes be used in addition to those given the experimental medication. Because the placebo "looks, tastes, or feels just like the actual treatment," the results are not skewed by what either group of patients think will happen. Thus, researchers can sometimes ensure that the results of taking the medicine are actually produced by it. (How are placebos used? section, ¶3)

  ☐ Acceptable use   ☐ Plagiarism

Potential use 4

As the American Cancer Society notes, "When there is no treatment approved for an illness, some people may be given a placebo . . ." (How are placebos used? section, ¶3). Other people will get the new treatment being tested. The reason for the placebo group is to be sure that whatever effects happen are actually caused by the treatment instead of some other thing. The placebo looks, tastes, or feels just like the actual treatment, so that by themselves, the patient's expectations will not determine the outcome.

☐ Acceptable use   ☐ Plagiarism

Potential use 5

In the Web posting, "Placebo Effect," the American Cancer Society (2009) explained that in an experimental treatment study, a control group might be given a placebo "to be sure that any effects that happen are actually caused by the treatment." Because the placebo is indistinguishable from the actual medicine, any results that might have been caused by anticipated effects are controlled (How are placebos used? section, ¶3).

☐ Acceptable use   ☐ Plagiarism

Potential use 6

In clinical trials, in addition to the patients who are given the experimental treatment, a placebo group might be employed in order to control for the effects of what the patients think will happen as a result of the treatment. Comparing the results of the treatment group with those of the placebo group allows the true effects of the treatment to be determined.

☐ Acceptable use   ☐ Plagiarism

6

Avoiding Plagiarism

It is the little writer rather than the great writer who never seems to quote, and the reason is that he is never really doing anything else.

—Havelock Ellis

An important part of using sources effectively lies in distinguishing between your own ideas and the ideas that come from outside sources. This chapter presents the information and guidelines you will need to know about what and when to cite so that you can avoid plagiarism, both intentional and unintentional.

- ◆ Learning about the various forms of plagiarism (intentional and unintentional) will enable you to avoid them.
- ◆ Committing intentional plagiarism harms the plagiarizer.
- ◆ Knowing what to cite makes citation easier.
- ◆ Learning about the myths surrounding citation will keep you from being deceived.

6.1 What is plagiarism?

In essence, plagiarism is a simple concept: When you make use of words, ideas, or any information from a source other than your own knowledge and experience, you must give credit to the source in a citation. Not giving credit to such borrowed intellectual material is plagiarism. There are a few complicating factors (such as *common knowledge*, discussed later on), but what appears to confuse the most people over this issue are uncertainties about the details and exceptions. Circulating on many campuses is a significant amount of wrong information about what needs to be cited and what constitutes appropriate citation.

A working definition of plagiarism

Perhaps the best way to clarify what plagiarism is (and is not) is to begin with a simple definition and then explain its meaning. Therefore, we will begin with this definition:

> **Plagiarism occurs when an information source is not properly credited.**

As you read and contemplate this brief definition, think about some of the implications. Specifically, note the following:

- ◆ **An information source includes much more than just words.** As you'll soon see, information sources include photographs, videos, and computer code.
- ◆ **Plagiarism is often unintentional.** Thus, it is not defined only as the *intentional* failure to credit an information source.

♦ **A source may be credited, but *improperly* credited.** Thus, there may still be plagiarism even though a citation is present.

♦ **Copyright is irrelevant.** The definition does not mention the legal status (copyright, public domain, permission to use, etc.) of the information because those elements are not relevant to the plagiarism issue.

♦ **The location and format of the source are irrelevant.** The source of the information (such as the Internet) has no bearing on the need to cite, nor does the form it takes—ink on paper, pixels on a screen, words spoken.

Intentional plagiarism

This is the kind of plagiarism most people think of when the subject is brought up: deliberate cheating on an assignment by copying a few sentences, a few paragraphs, or even an entire paper without quoting or citing the source. It is no secret to students—or to their instructors—that entire research papers are available both free and for sale on the Web, that journal articles can be copied from electronic databases, and that some students share their papers with each other. And, of course, every instructor knows how some students copy sentences and paragraphs from far and near and paste them into their papers without attribution.

This behavior, which amounts to stealing someone else's words and ideas and lying to the instructor by claiming them as the student's own, is highly offensive—to the instructor, who is taking the time to read the paper as if it were genuine; to other students, who are competing with what might be a professionally written work; and to the academy, whose degree is in danger of being awarded under false circumstances. Such complete disrespect for the academic enterprise (contempt for classmates, instructors, and academic integrity) is therefore punished harshly in most cases. A failing grade on the assignment is usually the most gentle penalty, with failure in the course more common. In higher education, expulsion from the college or university—together with a "cheating F" recorded on the student's permanent transcript—is not at all uncommon. That said, there are better reasons to avoid intentional plagiarism than merely the fear of punishment.

ACTIONS THAT CONSTITUTE PLAGIARISM

Downloading and turning in a paper from the Web, including a Web page or a paper mill essay	Including a graph, table, or picture from a source without proper citation
Copying and pasting phrases, sentences, or paragraphs into your paper without showing a quotation and adding proper citation	Getting so much help from a tutor or writing helper that the paper or part of the paper is no longer honestly your own work
Paraphrasing or summarizing a source's words or ideas without proper citation	Turning in previously written work when that practice is prohibited by your instructor

---

Unintentional plagiarism

Recall that our definition states, "Plagiarism occurs when an information source is not properly credited." The definition does not say whether or not the writer *intended* to provide proper credit. Thus, it is possible to commit plagiarism without intent. The causes of unintentional plagiarism are several, such as lack of knowledge of proper source use, misunderstanding the rules for citation, careless note taking, reliance on un-informed opinion about citing, and carelessness in the application of the rules of citation.

Sometimes, a significant source of unintentional plagiarism is the overuse or im-proper use of a tutor or editor. Be careful not to cross the line between getting advice and having a tutor contribute to your paper without acknowledgment. Writing tutors should not write sentences for you or make major changes to your own work. You may want to check institutional policy here, especially if you have a friend help you with your papers.

Self-recycling

Self-recycling involves a student's use of his or her own writing. Common examples include using a paper from a previous course in another course, turning in the same paper to two different instructors during the same term, or using portions of previously written work in new work. In surveys taken at the university level, most students be-lieved that self-recycling was permissible, thinking, "You can't plagiarize yourself." However, many professors and their institutions disagree. The purpose of a writing as-signment is not simply to create busy work that you can reduce by recycling previous work. Rather, the writing assignment provides you with an opportunity to explore a subject, hone your research skills, improve your thinking and analyzing abilities, prac-tice your writing skills — and learn a lot. Remember this:

> **The goal of education is not to get through, but to get better.**

Copying and pasting your own previous work short-circuits this intention just as effec-tively as copying and pasting text from somewhere else. For this reason, self-recycling and multiple submissions of papers are usually prohibited. If you have questions about self-recycling or multiple submission of papers, consult your instructor or ask about in-stitutional policy.

6.2 Why you should avoid intentional plagiarism

Many of the materials in this book will help you avoid unintentional plagiarism by training you in the proper use of sources: when to cite, how to cite, and how to build sources into your writing, both correctly and effectively. Avoiding intentional plagia-rism, on the other hand, must be a matter of personal choice on your part. If you are wondering why you should not cheat, consider the following points:

Intentional plagiarism harms your character

Would you like to have a friend who is a thief and a liar, acts pridefully superior to others, and takes advantage of others' honesty? Those who turn in the work of another as their own are doing exactly that. First, they steal another's words or ideas; then they lie about it by claiming authorship for them. Next, they turn in the paper, knowing that the instructor will expend pointless time and effort grading a paper and making com-ments that will have no effect on the students' learning. Last, they secretly sneer at those students who have made the effort to write their own paper, and, if the course is based on a curve, may actually harm the honest students' grades.

The fact is, our character is shaped by what we do. The person who cheats on research papers is rapidly losing personal integrity, and that loss will be reflected in other areas of life as well. For this reason, one of the most important results of formal education is who you become. Knowledge is important, and developing skills (such as thinking and writing) is important. But becoming a person of integrity—someone who can be trusted, someone who tells the truth—is indeed crucial. The habits you develop in college are likely to stay with you throughout your working life.

Follow the Golden Rule

Many writers, religious leaders, and philosophers have advocated the Golden Rule, "Behave toward others the same way you want them to behave toward you," because this rule helps hold the fabric of society together. If you cheat and others cheat, how will anyone ever be able to trust anyone else? Would you want to have heart surgery by a doctor who cheated through medical school? Would you want an attorney who cheated through law school? Would you even want an auto mechanic who cheated on the licensing exams? If you think it is all right for you to cheat, why should others do differently?

Intentional plagiarizers cheat themselves

Chapter 1 discussed the importance of learning how to write and think because most people will need these skills in whatever career they choose. Turning in a copied paper or even a paper assembled from copied parts prevents the development of these writing, thinking, and problem-solving skills as well as the skills of researching, organizing, planning, and attention to detail—all of which are highly valued by those who hire and promote employees. Thus, by not learning how to work with information in an economy based on working with information, intentional plagiarizers are cheating themselves out of future success. They also cheat themselves out of a significant part of their education by not gaining the knowledge and insights that researching and writing a paper would have given them.

6.3 Guidelines for citation

The definition of plagiarism at the beginning of this chapter tells us that an *information source* must be cited. An information source refers to any producer of information other than your own observation, knowledge, or experience. This idea can be expressed in another way as a working rule for citation:

> **If the information came from outside your own head, cite the source.**

The term *information* here will be interpreted quite broadly. The following sections will clarify the rule.

What needs to be cited?

The rather broad word *information* is used in the definitions above because breadth is needed to include all the forms of borrowed intellectual material (to use an even broader term) now available to you. The early definitions of plagiarism and the rules for citation used terms such as *borrowed words or ideas*, but phrases like this are clearly too limiting. The table below shows many kinds of intellectual property or information products in need of citation when you make use of them in your research papers. The list is not intended to be exhaustive, but rather to allow you to see the breadth of possibility. The following sections provide further guidelines.

WHAT TO CITE

You must cite someone else's
- words you quote
- words you summarize
- words you paraphrase
- idea (interpretation, opinion, conclusion)
- data
- graph
- photograph
- drawing
- table of information
- computer program code
- experiment
- survey
- example
- unique concept
- apt phrase (e.g., "flat-tire thinking")
- expression of common knowledge
- solution to a problem
- speech or audio recording
- video source (film, TV program)
- the structure or sequencing of facts, ideas, or arguments (e.g., from an encyclopedia)

You do not have to cite your own
- words
- idea (interpretation, opinion, conclusion)
- data
- graph
- photograph
- drawing
- table of information
- computer program code
- experiment
- survey
- example
- unique concept
- apt phrase
- expression of common knowledge
- solution to a problem

Remember: The *location* of the information source (such as the Web, a speech, or a book) and the *format* of the information (printed, digital, audio, video, live person) are irrelevant. You must cite all of the sources of information that you use, regardless of location or format.

What about common knowledge?

There is one exception to the rule of citing all outside information. Common knowledge does not need to be cited. Common knowledge includes whatever an educated person would be expected to know or could locate in an ordinary encyclopedia. It represents the kind of general information found in many sources and remembered by many people. Here are some of the types of common knowledge:

♦ **Easily observable information.** For example, heat makes people tired in summer; puppies display tremendous energy; most teenagers like chocolate; mud can be very sticky; certain types of trees lose their leaves in the fall; the First Amendment to the U. S. Constitution concerns freedom of speech and religion; the freeways are crowded at rush hour in many large cities.

♦ **Commonly reported facts.** For example, poet George Herbert was born in 1593 and died in 1633; Napoleon's army was decimated by the winter march on Moscow during the War of 1812; the Concorde passenger jet was developed jointly by the British and French; automobile tires are made from rubber compounds; cigarette smoking can cause health problems.

♦ **Common sayings.** For example, traditional proverbs need no citation: "Waste not, want not"; "Look before you leap"; "He who hesitates is lost." Some quotations have become proverbial as well, such as Alexander Pope's "Fools rush in where angels fear to tread." (Quoting more than this commonly spoken line would require a citation.)

There are some cautions to the above:

♦ **Finding the same information in several places does not automatically make it common knowledge.** Especially on the Web, information gets posted and reposted on many sites. A dozen sites selling the same vitamins or advancing the same political ideas may all have the same information, but that does not make the information common knowledge (or even reliable). Commonly expressed claims (that may be controversial) are not the same as common knowledge. Common knowledge means just that: generally accepted information of a factual or historical nature.

♦ **Quoting a source presenting common knowledge requires citation.** While common knowledge by itself need not be cited, *the source of the specific expression of common knowledge must be identified.* For example, you may mention without citation, as above, that Napoleon's army suffered ruinous losses during the march on Moscow. However, if your source says, "Napoleon's army froze in droves as it struggled ever so futilely toward Moscow," you must use quotation marks and cite the source of those words, if you use them. Therefore, if you use someone's words, you must quote and cite them, even if they contain an idea that is common knowledge.

♦ **An organized body of common knowledge needs citation.** A fact or two of common knowledge taken from an encyclopedia need not be cited. However, you may not summarize or paraphrase long passages without citation because the structure of information (its sequencing, emphasis, and selection) is not common knowledge and will need attribution.

♦ **Common knowledge is often intermingled with interpretation.** In many sources, common knowledge facts are mixed with analysis, interpretation, and opinion. All such commentary on common knowledge must be cited. For example, if your source says that operating the space shuttle program is an expensive project, that would not need citation, since it is common knowledge. However, if your source uses the word *wasteful* instead of (or in addition to) *expensive*, that is interpretation and would need citation.

♦ **You may not always know what is common knowledge.** When you encounter a fact that you believe might be common knowledge, but you are unsure, follow the rule of uncertainty:

> **If in doubt, cite it.**

It is much better to cite unnecessarily than to neglect citing something that should have been cited. If you have a large amount of common knowledge, such as some biographical details of a famous writer, it may be easier to paraphrase or summarize a single source (and cite it) than to assemble the many pieces from various general references.

♦ **Sometimes common knowledge sources disagree.** General sources may differ about the dates of certain events, the number of people involved, or even the definition of a term. If you are aware of such disagreement, you should cite the source you use or use and cite both (or all) pieces of conflicting information.

♦ **Common knowledge is not always true.** Sometimes, what "everybody knows" is not even correct. For example, the common belief that people should drink eight glasses of water a day is more myth than fact. The claim looks like a piece of common knowledge because it is repeated everywhere, yet there appears to be no scientific basis for it. Unless you are quite certain about a claim being both common and correct, you might want to cite the source or perform further research to resolve the issue.

This section can be summed up by the following decision tree, which helps you decide when to cite by asking just two questions:

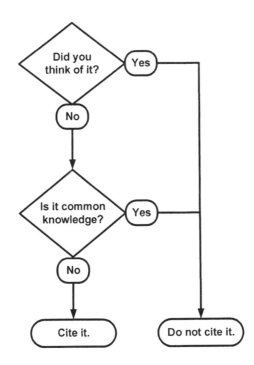

When Should You Cite?

Will my paper be nothing but citations?

A common fear or objection to the rule that all borrowed information must be cited is that such a practice will make the student's paper nothing but citations. However, as we noted in Chapter 1, sources and their citations support your own thinking and analysis. Your assignment is to *write* a research paper, not to *glue together* a research paper by using a few transitional expressions to connect a handful of sources. Much of the paper should consist of your own thinking, analysis, interpretation, examples, commentary, fresh ideas, judgments, explanations, anecdotes, evaluation of data, and so on.

Do you ever have to cite yourself?

The surprising answer is, Yes. If you have created a previous work, such as an experiment you performed and wrote up, a short film, survey analysis, formal speech, and so on, you must cite it if you quote or refer to it in a new work. If you perform the experiment for the paper you are working on, then you do not cite it. Whatever you have written or created before becomes a potential source that you then should cite when you borrow from it. Yes, you can even quote yourself (though, of course, discretion is advised). An exception to this rule would be a case where an instructor allows you to make use of previous work to generate new work, as in taking an old paper and revising it into a new paper, or using sections of previous work in a new work.

A final reason for self-citation is to clarify the source of an illustration. It is assumed that tables, graphs, charts, and descriptive drawings have been produced by the writer of the paper (unless otherwise cited). However, photographs and artistic drawings might be less clearly understood as the paper writer's work, because not every writer is a photographer or artist. In order to avoid confusion, then, it might prove helpful to add a note such as "Photograph by the author" to such work. If your paper includes photographs both by you and by other sources, it becomes essential to add personal credit or an appropriate citation to each.

6.4 Myths and facts about citing

This section is intended to clear up many of the misconceptions about the use of various kinds of information available to you, by exposing and correcting some of the myths about citing. A myth in the sense used here means a wrong belief, often spread around commonly by others who do not know the facts.

The public domain myth

Myth: You can quote anything that is in the public domain or no longer protected by copyright without having to cite the source.

Fact: As mentioned above, the legal status of a piece of information has no bearing on whether or not it needs to be cited. Words, ideas, or other kinds of information taken from a source must be cited, whether the information is copyrighted or in the public domain. Do not confuse information that is in the public domain with information that is common knowledge. Public domain information is now owned by the public, so that no royalties need be paid for its reproduction. However, most of this information is not common knowledge, so the source of any borrowed words or ideas from this public domain material must still be cited.

PLAGIARISM AND COPYRIGHT INFRINGEMENT

Plagiarism and copyright infringement both refer to violations of intellectual property standards, but the two violations are different. Plagiarism is an ethical violation relating to a lack of proper attribution for borrowed material. Copyright infringement is a legal violation relating to the misuse of intellectual property, usually for financial gain. The differences can be clarified by the following example. Imagine that I start a publishing company called Bob's Press and I publish the four books below.

Gulliver's Travels by Jonathan Swift **Published by Bob's Press**	**Gulliver's Travels by Robert Harris** **Published by Bob's Press**	**The Hunt for Red October by Tom Clancy** **Published by Bob's Press**	**The Hunt for Red October by Robert Harris** **Published by Bob's Press**
Not Plagiarism Not Copyright Infringement	Plagiarism but Not Copyright Infringement	Copyright Infringement but Not Plagiarism	Copyright Infringement and Plagiarism

The first book, *Gulliver's Travels* by Jonathan Swift, is in the public domain because it was first published in 1726 and all copyrights have long since expired. So I can publish this book or parts of it without copyright infringement. Further, as long as I accurately attribute the text I publish to its real author, I do not commit plagiarism. In fact, I might be considered a respected publisher of classic literature.

The second book, however, commits plagiarism because now I am claiming to be the author of a work that I did not write. I am still not guilty of copyright infringement, though, since the book is not copyrighted.

The third book, *The Hunt for Red October* by Tom Clancy, accurately lists its real author, so I am not guilty of plagiarism by reprinting it. However, Mr. Clancy's publisher would be highly upset if I did so, because I would be guilty of copyright infringement. The book is still copyrighted and I do not have the rights to print the book. My printing it, then, would most likely see me hauled into court, ordered to cease distributing it, and required to pay monetary damages.

The fourth book would commit both plagiarism and copyright infringement because it claims that I am the author of a work I did not write (plagiarism) and it unlawfully uses copyrighted intellectual property (copyright infringement).

The fair use myth

Myth: Even if a work is copyrighted, I can use it without attribution because I have *fair use* under copyright law.

Fact: This myth arises from a confusion similar to that above. Fair use allows you to quote a source without payment or written permission. (For example, you can quote a dozen lines from a copyrighted poem in order to analyze it in a paper you are writing for a class, without having to pay the copyright holder a royalty.) Fair use, however, does not permit you to steal the author's words by claiming them as your own. In fact, as we have just seen in the example on the previous page, if you do plagiarize a copyrighted source, you may be guilty not only of plagiarism (an academic dishonesty offense) but also of copyright infringement (a civil, and in some cases criminal, offense).

The World Wide Web myth

Myth: Whatever is on the Web is common knowledge, so it is permissible to use anything there without quotation marks or attribution.

Fact: This myth contains two errors. First, much of the information on the Web is not common knowledge. The Web is filled with unique facts, interpretations, opinions, commentaries, creative works, original articles, and much more. The second error lies in not recognizing that even what is common knowledge on the Web or elsewhere cannot be quoted word-for-word without citation. *The quotation of any words from a source needs to have quotation marks (or a block quotation) and a citation.* And recall that the "expression of common knowledge" needs to be cited.

It should also be noted in relation to this myth that most of what is on the Web is also copyrighted. Web pages, letters, e-mail, and other forms of written communication are now automatically copyrighted as soon as they are written down. It is no longer necessary to register writing with the copyright office in order to be protected. And note that copyright also applies to photographs, drawings, and other intellectual property on the Web.

The encyclopedia myth

Myth: Because encyclopedias contain common or general knowledge, I can copy from them without having to cite them.

Fact: While it is true that common knowledge (such as the dates of birth and death of Abraham Lincoln, or the names of the fifty states) does not need attribution, quoting an encyclopedia (which may not be a very scholarly practice anyway) does require attribution and quotation marks for two reasons. First, *whenever* you copy words, you must use quotation marks or a block indentation (and a citation in each case) to show that you are quoting.

Second, there is much more in encyclopedias than common knowledge facts. Attribution is required for any source (including encyclopedias) from which you get judgments, conclusions, viewpoints, interpretations, thoughts, ideas, evaluations, specific words or phrases, findings, controversial facts, or even interesting questions. As mentioned earlier, the best rule to follow here is, "If in doubt, cite it." Even if you think you have an item of common knowledge, reference its source. Overcitation is never a vice; undercitation is never a virtue.

The paraphrased paper myth

Myth: If I change a common knowledge source into my own words, I can use the whole source without attribution.

Fact: As we discussed in the previous chapter on paraphrasing, the structure and sequence of ideas are considered unique to the writer and are therefore not common knowledge. You can use a fact or two from a common knowledge source without citation, but to copy the same structure and order of facts, even in your own words, would be to commit plagiarism. If you think about it for a moment, you will see that if the wholesale paraphrasing of common knowledge were allowed, it would defeat the purpose of writing research papers because students would be merely replacing words rather than performing the tasks of researching, analyzing, and integrating sources into their own writing.

The friend's permission myth

Myth: If my friend gives me permission to use his or her paper, I can turn it in as my own without being guilty of plagiarism, because I am not stealing my friend's words or ideas.

Fact: If you are writing an academic research paper, there is no circumstance where you are permitted to present the words of another as your own. (Even if you are writing a paper as a team, you are claiming that the team is the true author of the words of the paper, except where items have been clearly quoted.) No source can elect not to be cited. Another way to say this is that no one can give you permission to deceive your instructor into thinking you wrote something you did not write. Even sources that want to remain anonymous must be cited—as anonymous sources.

The named source myth

Myth: If I mention the author's name in the text, I can copy word-for-word and quotation marks are not necessary.

Fact: Remember that a fundamental goal of including research material from others is to differentiate between your ideas and the words and ideas of your sources. All quotations require either quotation marks or block indentations. All text in your paper without one of these is assumed to have been written by you. If that assumption is wrong, you are plagiarizing.

The converted words myth

Myth: If I turn the source's words completely into my own words, then the words and ideas become my own, and I do not need to cite the source.

Fact: You cannot write a source out of existence by changing words around. Putting a source's words completely into your own words is an effective strategy known as paraphrasing. Yet every paraphrase must be cited because every source must be cited. The origin of *ideas* as well as words needs proper attribution. The applicable saying here is, "Give credit where credit is due."

The tiny theft myth

Myth: If I use only a few words from a source, I don't need to cite them.

Fact: Every quoted word needs to be cited (as well as placed in quotation marks). The best example of quoting just a few words is the *apt phrase*, two or three words that provide a flair or flavor from a source. Sometimes the phrase is simply unusual or artistic, as in an alliteration such as "clandestine coup." Often, the apt phrase is a colorful metaphor, as in "pretzeled logic." Whatever the case, borrowed words must be quoted and cited. The temptation to steal another writer's wit or rhetorical elegance can sometimes be great: resist it.

The background information myth

Myth: I just used the source for background information but did not actually cite any part of it, so all I needed to do was list the source in the bibliography.

Fact: If you use information from a source in your paper, you must cite where you use it. Any item of background information you mention must be cited unless it is common knowledge. Remember that a use includes paraphrase, summary, brief mention, or even an isolated fact, not just a quotation or direct reference to the author's interpretation. If the source contained only common knowledge that you therefore did not cite, do not list the source in the bibliography. The References list (APA) and Works Cited list (MLA) should contain only those works explicitly referred to in your paper.

THE GOLDEN TEST

You can avoid worrying about all the myths above by relying instead on a simple test for deciding whether or not you need to cite a piece of information. Ask the question, "Will my reader likely believe that this information originated with me when it did not?" If the answer is "Yes," then you need a citation to correct your reader's misunderstanding.

Review questions

To see how well you understand this chapter, attempt to answer each of the following questions without referring to the text. (Write down your answers to make checking easier.) Then check your answers with the text. If you missed something important, add it to your answer.

1. In your own words, define *plagiarism.*

2. Describe the difference between intentional and unintentional plagiarism.

3. What is *self-recycling,* and why do most academic institutions prohibit it?

4. How do intentional plagiarizers hurt themselves?

5. Give examples of information sources *other than words* that must be cited.

6. Define *common knowledge* and give an example.

7. Explain the relationship between plagiarism and copyright infringement.

Questions for thought and discussion

Use these questions for in-class or small-group discussion, or for stimulating your own thinking.

1. Have you ever been falsely accused of plagiarism? If so, how did you defend yourself?

2. Has this chapter convinced you that self-recycling is not in your own best interest? Why or why not?

3. After reading this chapter, do you think you might have inadvertently plagiarized in the past? What form did it take? Do you now feel able to avoid accidental plagiarism in the future?

4. Before reading this chapter, were you misled by any of the myths about citing? Do you now understand why they are indeed myths?

Name _____   Course _____

Chapter 6 Review: True-false quiz

Directions: In each case, determine whether the statement is true or false.

1. It is **not** possible to plagiarize something in the public domain.
   ☐ True   ☐ False

2. It is possible to commit plagiarism by accident.
   ☐ True   ☐ False

3. You cannot plagiarize yourself.
   ☐ True   ☐ False

4. You do *not* have to cite quoted common knowledge.
   ☐ True   ☐ False

5. Everything on the Web is in the public domain.
   ☐ True   ☐ False

6. Even if you turn a quotation entirely into your own words, you still have to cite the source.
   ☐ True   ☐ False

7. It is *not* plagiarism to turn in your friend's paper as your own if you have your friend's permission to do so.
   ☐ True   ☐ False

8. If you copy and paste a photograph from a Web site into your paper, you must provide a citation for the photograph.
   ☐ True   ☐ False

9. You do *not* need to cite fewer than five quoted words.
   ☐ True   ☐ False

10. You can use a source, add a citation, and still be guilty of plagiarism.
    ☐ True   ☐ False

Name _____   Course _____

Chapter 6: Rules of citation quiz

Directions: In each case, decide whether you must include a citation of the source for the information described.

1. In a book, you find the phrase "cultural tapeworm" and want to use it in your paper.
   ☐ Have to cite it   ☐ Do not have to cite it

2. You conduct a personal interview with a doctor to get information about treatment for skin rashes. You make your own notes. In your paper, you use information from the interview.
   ☐ Have to cite it   ☐ Do not have to cite it

3. You read in several different sources about how online day traders in the stock market have turned stock buying and selling into a form of recreational gambling. In your paper, you mention in your own words that for some people the stock market seems to have become another kind of gambling.
   ☐ Have to cite it   ☐ Do not have to cite it

4. You create and distribute a survey to shoppers at a mall, asking about the brands of clothing they prefer. You include a table of the results in your paper.
   ☐ Have to cite it   ☐ Do not have to cite it

5. In your paper, you write, "Neil Armstrong set foot on the moon." This is a fact you have read many times in the past and you now do not remember where.
   ☐ Have to cite it   ☐ Do not have to cite it

6. In a paperback almanac published last year, you locate a graph showing the historical rise of energy consumption in the United States. You include this graph in your paper.
   ☐ Have to cite it   ☐ Do not have to cite it

7. In your paper, you paraphrase but do not quote a federal government document that is not copyrighted.
   ☐ Have to cite it   ☐ Do not have to cite it

8. You decide to end your paper with a bit of ancient wisdom, so you quote the traditional old proverb, "Look before you leap."
   ☐ Have to cite it   ☐ Do not have to cite it

9. You are writing a paper on childbirth. On a Web page, you locate a photograph of a baby in its mother's arms and paste the photograph into your paper.
   ☐ Have to cite it   ☐ Do not have to cite it

10. You locate a brilliant argument in favor of an idea you are advancing in a paper. You decide to use this argument but turn it completely into your own words.
   ☐ Have to cite it   ☐ Do not have to cite it

Notes

7
Putting It Together

Have you ever observed that we pay much more attention to a wise passage when it is quoted than when we read it in the original author?
—Philip G. Hamerton

Now that you know how to select and prepare your sources for use in your research paper, there remains the task of putting everything together in a way that makes your writing clear and effective. Your sources should be smoothly built into the flow of your paper and yet clearly distinguished from your own writing. This chapter explains how to integrate your sources with your own words.

- ♦ Applying the Simple Rule by marking the boundaries of your source will clearly identify the words and ideas you have borrowed from a source.
- ♦ Marking the boundaries also helps to give you credit for your own ideas by clearly differentiating them from those of a source.
- ♦ Citing borrowed tables and graphics is important, also, and is too often forgotten.

7.1 The Simple Rule: Mark the boundaries

The Simple Rule for incorporating sources into your writing is *Mark the boundaries*. The rule is a reminder to distinguish carefully between your own words and ideas and those of the sources you use. Simply stated, you place boundary markers around the source material you use to set it off from your own writing. In other words, you indicate clearly when you begin to draw upon a source and when you have finished. The source material is framed or enclosed by the use of boundary markers.

Marking the boundaries of your sources also has the practical value of helping you avoid plagiarism, because you show clearly when you are using research material. But just as important, the boundary markers show your reader which ideas are your own.

Marking the boundaries of short quotations

When you use an author's exact words, marking the boundaries involves using quotation marks for quotations of fewer than four lines or fewer than forty words. In addition to the quotation marks, the markers include an introductory lead-in and a citation.

MARKING THE BOUNDARIES OF SHORT QUOTATIONS
(a short phrase, part of a sentence, an entire sentence, or two or three sentences)

Boundaries are marked by
① a lead-in, ② opening and closing quotation marks, and ③ a citation

---

Example 7.1.1
Phrase, APA:
Doe (2007) argued that history is "an interpretation of selected events" rather than a mere presentation of facts (p. 131).

Phrase, MLA:
John Doe argues that history is "an interpretation of selected events" rather than a mere presentation of facts (131).

Example 7.1.2
Part of a sentence, APA:
The practice of bloodletting to cure disease, wrote Doe (2006), was derived from "the medieval theory of the four humours, which supposed that many ailments arose from an excess of blood in need of reducing to its proper level" (p. 224).

Part of a sentence, MLA:
The practice of bloodletting to cure disease, writes Jane Doe, was derived from "the medieval theory of the four humours, which supposed that many ailments arose from an excess of blood in need of reducing to its proper level" (224).

Example 7.1.3
Entire sentence, APA:
Doe (2009) viewed the site as a probable burial pit: "The artifacts of the L2 site were all bunched together within a rough circle approximately three meters in diameter" (p. 233).

Entire sentence, MLA:
Jane Doe views the site as a probable burial pit: "The artifacts of the L2 site were all bunched together within a rough circle approximately three meters in diameter" (233).

In all of these examples, the author's words are clearly marked and attributed. This boundary marking separates the source information from your own ideas and words.

Marking the boundaries for long quotations

When you quote at length, the words are set off from the rest of the text using a block indentation that visually shows the boundaries of the quoted words. No quotation marks are needed because the visual separation clearly shows the quotation. An introductory lead-in prepares the reader for the long quotation, and a citation ends it.

MARKING THE BOUNDARIES OF LONG QUOTATIONS
(more than four lines [MLA] or 40 words [APA] or one or more paragraphs)

Boundaries are marked by
① a lead-in, ② a block indentation, and ③ a citation

Example 7.1.4
Paragraph, APA (indent one-half inch):
Maheu and Gordon (2000) suggested that even as online technologies are being used in-

creasingly for counseling and therapy purposes, these new modes of contact need to be assessed carefully:

> Each interactive technology raises new concerns related to its particular strengths and limitations. For instance, the use of videoconferencing involves both similar and different issues than does E-mail interaction with patients. Each technology needs to be examined separately for its related risk management issues. Likewise, each patient should be assessed for the need for and the suitability of on-line services, should be clearly informed of the nature and the limitations of the services, and should be given plans for possible equipment failures and crises. (p. 487)

Paragraph, MLA (indent ten spaces or one inch):
Marlene Maheu and Barry Gordon suggest that even as online technologies are being used increasingly for counseling and therapy purposes, these new modes of contact need to be assessed carefully:

> Each interactive technology raises new concerns related to its particular strengths and limitations. For instance, the use of videoconferencing involves both similar and different issues than does E-mail interaction with patients. Each technology needs to be examined separately for its related risk management issues. Likewise, each patient should be assessed for the need for and the suitability of on-line services, should be clearly informed of the nature and the limitations of the services, and should be given plans for possible equipment failures and crises. (487)

Comment:
Note that for both APA and MLA block quotation style, there are no quotation marks and the parenthetical citation floats after the final period. These are two differences from in-text quotations, where there are quotation marks and where the parenthetical citation is punctuated as part of the last sentence.

Marking the boundaries of an unquoted source

When you rely on source material without quoting it, there are no quotation marks (or block indent), so the introductory lead-in and a close (often a citation) are even more important because they alone function as the boundary markers.

MARKING THE BOUNDARIES OF AN UNQUOTED SOURCE
(summarizing, paraphrasing, mentioning briefly, or using an idea from the source)

Boundaries are marked by
① a lead-in, and ② a citation or other close

Your reader must be able to distinguish between your own ideas and arguments and those of the sources you use. Boundary markers are the only way to be clear about this.

A paragraph that consists of a dozen or so lines of text with a citation only at the beginning or end is unfortunately common in some students' research papers. In this type of paragraph, there is no indication how much of the paragraph draws upon the source mentioned in the citation. Does the citation apply to the whole paragraph or only the sentence containing the citation? Or does the writer intend it to apply to two or three sentences but not to all? Without both boundary markers, the citation alone can be confusing. Study the examples below to understand this problem more clearly and to learn how to remedy it.

Example 7.1.5
Source:
When a consumer product is subject to a recall order, it seldom travels anywhere. The order means that an identified fault must be remedied by the manufacturer. The remedy often involves only the mailing of new parts to the consumer or a visit to a repair center. —Jane Doe, 2008, p. 456

Hypothetical student paragraph with citation, APA style:
A product recall might be more accurately known as a product repair because most recalled products never leave the consumer's home. In many cases, when a defect is discovered by the manufacturer, a repair kit is sent to the consumer. In other cases, the product must be taken in for repair. Rarely will the product be called in and exchanged for another. For example, recalled automobiles are never returned to the factory and replaced; they are simply repaired at a dealer (Doe, 2008, p. 456).

Hypothetical student paragraph with citation, MLA style:
A product recall might be more accurately known as a product repair because most recalled products never leave the consumer's home. In many cases, when a defect is discovered by the manufacturer, a repair kit is sent to the consumer. In other cases, the product must be taken in for repair. Rarely will the product be called in and exchanged for another. For example, recalled automobiles are never returned to the factory and replaced; they are simply repaired at a dealer (Doe 456).

Comment:
In the paragraphs shown above, the student has not distinguished original ideas from a paraphrase of Doe. Neither an instructor nor any other reader will be able to tell how much of the paragraph is being attributed to the source. Note below the proper use of boundary markers.

Paragraph with boundary markers, APA style:
A product recall might be more accurately known as a product repair. As Doe (2008) noted, most recalled products never leave the consumer's home. In many cases, when a defect is discovered by the manufacturer, a repair kit is sent to the consumer. In other cases, the product must be taken in for repair. Rarely will the product be called in and exchanged for another (p. 456). For example, recalled automobiles are never returned to the factory and replaced; they are simply repaired at a dealer.

Paragraph with boundary markers, MLA style:
A product recall might be more accurately known as a product repair. As Jane Doe notes, most recalled products never leave the consumer's home. In many cases, when a defect is discovered by the manufacturer, a repair kit is sent to the consumer. In other cases, the product must be taken in for repair. Rarely will the product be called in and exchanged for another (456). For example, recalled automobiles are never returned to the factory and replaced; they are simply repaired at a dealer.

The use of both boundary markers in the above two examples shows that the first part of the paragraph (renaming a recall to a repair) is the student's own idea, as is the example of the automobile recall at the end of the paragraph. Thus, including the proper boundary markers where they belong not only sets off the source but also clearly reveals the student's own ideas in the paragraph. Once again, *your own thinking is important*: It is a significant part of what your instructor expects. Give yourself credit, and be sure to show the difference between your ideas and those you are incorporating from research.

7.2 Marking the boundaries in problem cases

Occasionally, situations arise when you must use a little creativity to construct your boundary markers. Example situations include these: (1) Web pages usually lack page numbers, (2) some Web pages show no author, and (3) citing an entire article or book in APA style does not require the use of page numbers. In these cases, there may be only one obvious item to use as a boundary marker.

Creating a second boundary marker

One solution for indicating an end boundary is to show clearly that new material is beginning. One of the following markers may be appropriate:

- ◆ Start a new paragraph.
- ◆ Add a clear transition of thought (for example, "Another researcher says").
- ◆ Show clearly that you are now commenting (for example, "But Doe does not mention"; "Doe's implication is clear, it seems, when").

Another solution is to use information about the source (author, title, subject, thesis, role in your paper) to create an additional marker. That way, the new marker serves to introduce the source and the citation information serves as the closing boundary marker.

Example 7.2.1
Problem passage, entire article cited, APA style:
Boolean logic frees the researcher from using only one keyword at a time. Doe (2008) reported that using the appropriate forms of Boolean logic allows the searcher to control both the breadth of the search and the desired proximity of the search terms. This type of precision is simply impossible with paper indexes or printed bibliographies.

Comment:
This passage shows clearly that the first sentence belongs to the writer of the paper, while the second belongs to Doe. However, it fails to show that the last sentence belongs to the writer rather than Doe because there is no terminating boundary marker. In this case, the solution to the problem is to construct a second boundary marker by describing the author of the source, as in the following example:

Improved passage, entire article cited, APA style:
Boolean logic frees the researcher from using only one keyword at a time. A Library of Congress researcher says that using the appropriate forms of Boolean logic allows the searcher to control both the breadth of the search and the desired proximity of the search terms (Doe, 2008). This type of precision is simply impossible with paper indexes or printed bibliographies.

Example 7.2.2
Problem passage, Web page with no stated author or date, APA style:
According to "Making Lighting Work" (n.d.), when room lighting is designed, more than just lighting intensity (or brightness) needs to be taken into account. The color of the light and the location of the sources are also critical. Without consideration of all these factors, glare, eyestrain, and bizarre shadows can result.

Note: For APA, use "n.d." for *no date*.

Improved passage, Web page with no stated author or date, APA style:
According to an article on the Lighting Institute Web site, when room lighting is designed, more than just lighting intensity (or brightness) needs to be taken into account. The color of the light and the location of the sources are also critical. Without consideration of all these factors, glare, eyestrain, and bizarre shadows can result ("Making Lighting Work," n.d.).

Improved passage, Web page with no stated author or date, MLA style:
According to an article on the Lighting Institute Web site, when room lighting is designed, more than just lighting intensity (or brightness) needs to be taken into account. The color of the light and the location of the sources are also critical. Without consideration of all these factors, glare, eyestrain, and bizarre shadows can result ("Making Lighting Work").

Comment:
These improved passages neatly package the source material so that the writer can now make comments before and after it in the same paragraph without creating any confusion in the reader's mind about whose ideas are being presented. Comments before the passage might provide a context for it. Then, after the passage, additional examples or discussion can be added. The result is a clear and coherent argument, supported by a well-integrated source.

Marking the boundaries for nontext information

You will recall from earlier chapters that *all borrowed information must be cited*, including photographs, drawings, tables, graphs, and so forth. The rules for citation are similar, taking into account the visual nature of the information.

Nontext information, such as a graph or table, sets itself off from your text by its visual form, much as a block indentation sets off a long, quoted text. Even so, this type of information includes boundary markers. For citation purposes, nontext information is divided into two categories: tables and figures. A table involves the presentation of words or data in a structured form. A figure includes a graph, a drawing, or a photograph.

In APA style, boundary markers for a table include a label at the beginning and a note with the citation at the end. If the table has been taken from a source exactly as it appears in the source, it is cited as *From*, but if you reorganize the data or take only part of it, the table is cited as *Adapted from*. (Note that for papers prepared for publication, a copyright notice naming the copyright holder of the source of the table is also included at the end of the bibliographic information, and if necessary a note that permission has been secured. See Example 7.2.5.)

Example 7.2.3
Table, APA style:

Table 3
Favorite Picnic Locations by Age

	< 15	15–34	35–50	> 50
Beach	52	31	25	22
Sunny lawn	40	48	31	17
Shaded tree	8	21	44	61

From "Recreational Options As Influenced by Climate and Age," by J. Doe, 2008, *Journal of Leisure Time, 43,* p. 274.

In MLA style, table boundary markers are very similar to APA style, with the same beginning marker of the word *Table*, a number, and a title on the line below. The ending marker is similar also, with the word *Source* replacing the word *From*. The citation, of course, is in MLA style.

Example 7.2.4
Table citation, MLA style

Table 6
Favorite Picnic Locations by Age[a]

	< 15	15–34	35–50	> 50
Beach	52	31	25	22
Sunny Lawn	40	48	31	17
Shaded Tree	8	21	44	61

Source: Jane Doe, "Recreational Options As Influenced by Climate and Age," *Journal of Leisure Time*, 43 (2008) 274. Print.
[a]Survey taken June 6, 2008. $n = 346$.

For figures (graphs, drawings, and photographs) in APA citation style, the graphic itself provides the beginning marker (like a block indent), so you need only the ending marker, which consists of a label and a citation. The label should include the word *Figure* and a figure number, and a title or caption for the figure.

Example 7.2.5
Figure, APA style, with copyright and permission notice:

Figure 12. Creative thinking stimulus drawing. From *Creative Problem Solving* (p. 100), by R. A. Harris, 2002, Los Angeles: Pyrczak Publishing. Copyright 2002 by Pyrczak Publishing. Reprinted with permission.

As with the table, if the graphic is pasted in exactly as it appears in the source, it is cited as *From*, but if you crop, enhance, or otherwise alter it, the graphic is cited as *Adapted from*. (As with a table, if your paper is being prepared for publication, include a copyright notice at the end of the bibliographic information.)

Once again, for MLA style, boundary markers are similar to those in APA. The graphic provides its own beginning marker and the citation at the end follows MLA style. Note that MLA abbreviates the figure label to *Fig.* and does not italicize it.

Example 7.2.6
Figure citation, MLA style:

Fig. 12. Creative Thinking Stimulus Drawing. From Robert A. Harris, *Creative Problem Solving* (Los Angeles: Pyrczak, 2002) 100. Print.

Review questions

To see how well you understand this chapter, attempt to answer each of the following questions without referring to the text. (Write down your answers to make checking easier.) Then check your answers with the text. If you missed something important, add it to your answer.

1. In your own words, define the Simple Rule.

2. Why is it important to indicate the beginning and ending of the sources used?

3. Describe several ways to create an introductory boundary marker when the usual bibliographic information for the source is limited, as for example with an anonymous Web article.

4. Describe several ways to create a second boundary marker when there is too little standard bibliographic information about the source.

Questions for thought and discussion

Use these questions for in-class or small-group discussion, or for stimulating your own thinking.

1. What might be the result if your reader cannot match one or more of your citations to an entry in the References or Works Cited page?

2. Do you think that the process of using boundary markers will help you avoid unintentional plagiarism? Why or why not?

3. Have you ever simply grabbed a photograph or drawing from the Web (using Google Image Search, perhaps) and inserted it into a paper without thinking about citing the source? What will you do from now on?

4. Does one of the citation styles covered in this chapter seem to be better or easier than the other? If so, explain why, using specific examples.

Name _____   Course _____

Chapter 7 Review: True-false quiz

Directions: In each case, determine whether the statement is true or false.

1. A lead-in at the beginning and a citation (such as a page number) or other type of close can form the boundary markers for a paraphrased source.
   ☐ True   ☐ False

2. If you don't have enough information about your source, such as a Web page with no author, you can omit the boundary markers.
   ☐ True   ☐ False

3. The boundary markers for a photograph taken from a source include a figure title and the bibliographic information from the source.
   ☐ True   ☐ False

4. If you alter the format of a table or figure, you must clearly indicate this change in your boundary marker by using the phrase *Adapted from.*
   ☐ True   ☐ False

5. Quotations of more than 40 words (APA) or four lines (MLA) should be indented and written as a block, with no quotation marks.
   ☐ True   ☐ False

6. Tables and graphics do not need to be surrounded by quotation marks because they are set off from the text by their form.
   ☐ True   ☐ False

7. If you are using a source without a date for an APA-style paper, you should put an "earlier than the current year" marker in the parentheses, as in "Jones (<2011)."
   ☐ True   ☐ False

8. Only quotations need two boundary markers, while paraphrases and summaries need only one marker.
   ☐ True   ☐ False

9. When you merely refer to an idea from a source, you can omit formal boundary markers and simply include the source in your References or Works Cited.
   ☐ True   ☐ False

10. If you are preparing your paper for publication and include a graphic from a source, you should add copyright information for the source.
   ☐ True   ☐ False

Name _____   Course _____

Chapter 7 Review: Boundary markers

Directions: For each example, decide whether or not the boundaries between the source use and the paper writer's own words have been adequately marked. In cases where the difference is not clear, suggest improvements. Finally, if the source is summarized or paraphrased, decide whether the use is properly constructed or commits plagiarism.

Source text

Initially, oil rigs were required to be directly over the reservoir of oil they sought to pump out. Later, however, the development of slant drilling techniques permitted oil companies to reach multiple crude sources from a single drilling location, such as an offshore platform. Onshore, slant drilling allowed the exploitation of resources beneath developed areas. —John Doe, 2010, p. 123

Potential use 1, APA style

In the early days of oil drilling, oil rigs were required to be directly over the reservoir of oil they sought to pump out. But then, as Doe (2010) wrote, "The development of slant drilling techniques permitted oil companies to reach multiple crude sources from a single drilling location, such as an offshore platform" (p. 123). On land, slant drilling allowed the use of resources beneath developed areas.

Potential use 2, APA style

Early oil rigs could drill only straight down, so that they had to be right on top of the pools of oil they tapped. Eventually, slant drilling enabled access to oil resources from locations far to the side of a given pool (Doe, 2010, p. 123).

Potential use 3, MLA style

Oil drilling has not always been as flexible as it is today. In the early days, as oil historian John Doe tells us, drilling rigs had to be "directly over the reservoir of oil they sought to pump out" (123).

Potential use 4, MLA style

In his discussion of the history of oil drilling, John Doe reminds us that the technique of slant drilling (drilling at an angle from a wellhead) was not available early on. Originally, the pool of oil to be tapped had to be directly under the wellhead. Only later could oil beneath settled land be tapped from the side, and multiple locations tapped from a single offshore rig (123).

Potential use 5, APA style

Originally, claimed Doe (2010), oil rigs had to be directly over the reservoir of oil they pumped. Later on, however, the invention of slant drilling procedures allowed oil companies to reach several oil sources from a single drilling spot, such as an offshore platform. On land, slant drilling permitted the drilling of oil beneath industrialized areas.

Notes

8
Effective Use

The power of quotation is as dreadful a weapon as any which the human intellect can forge.
—John Jay Chapman

Previous chapters have shown you how to select, prepare, and incorporate sources into your research-based writing. This chapter takes you a step further by providing some practical techniques for enhancing your use of sources to help you make your researched writing particularly effective.

♦ Introducing your sources more fully will give them greater credibility.
♦ Discussing the meaning or implications of the source clarifies its purpose and impact.
♦ Blending your sources into your writing will make your writing stronger.
♦ Avoiding the common pitfalls of ineffective source use will help you maintain your readers' confidence in your writing.

8.1 Introduce the source thoroughly

Section 4.2 of Chapter 4 discussed general strategies for introducing your sources. The discussion here provides you with some more advanced introductory strategies that will help you add attention and credibility to the sources you use.

Establish the credibility of the source

Going back at least to the time of ancient Greek and Roman oratory, speakers have traditionally been introduced, often by someone familiar to the audience, to attest to their trustworthiness. Ever since printed books have become available, prefaces and forewords by well-known people often recommend the books (and their authors) to the public. Your role as the introducer of a source is similar. When you say, "As John Doe says," your reader's first reaction might be to ask a few questions:

♦ Who is this John Doe?
♦ Why is he being quoted (or summarized or paraphrased)?
♦ Why should I believe him, anyway?
♦ What is this reference doing here?

In other words, your role as introducer of a source is to provide the reader with enough background that the source appears to be worth paying attention to as a credible voice. You will recall that the first test of source evaluation, discussed in Chapter 2, Section 2.5, is *Expertise*. Now that you have located a source that has met the criteria for expertise, you may wish to offer some of the evidence of this expertise to your reader. Note the difference:

♦ As John Doe says, "These South American plants are dangerous."

♦ As John Doe, some guy with a Web page, says, "These South American plants are dangerous."

♦ As John Doe, author of *Poisonous Plants of South America*, says, "These South American plants are dangerous."

Clearly, the information provided in the last instance gives the reader much more reason to accept John Doe's comments as authoritative than does the information in the introductory language of the first two. The background information that helps build credibility of an author includes the following:

♦ organizational affiliation (for example, of the Mayo Clinic)

♦ respected Web site (for example, a government site: FDA, FTC, FBI, etc.)

♦ job description (for example, coroner, geologist, forensic chemist, automotive safety engineer, market analyst)

♦ relevant publications (name the one you are citing or another one that establishes an arena of expertise)

♦ relevant accomplishments (for example, war veteran, mountaineer, Nobel laureate, eyewitness)

♦ relevant experience (for example, twenty years' experience spotting art fakes)

Two words of caution are appropriate here. First, avoid making a bald authority appeal, which implies that a writer should be believed just because he or she possesses expert credentials or is associated with a famous organization. (See the fallacy of appeal to prestige in Section 8.5 later in this chapter.) The credentials tell us why we should listen to the source, but the quality of the source's arguments and evidence is what persuades us (or not) about the issue at hand. Second, use these introductions somewhat sparingly and keep them fairly brief, in order to keep the focus on the information under discussion rather than on the credentials.

Another way to establish credibility is to comment on the nature of the information itself, showing that the way it was acquired makes it likely to be dependable:

♦ In a major national survey, Doe (2006) discovered that

♦ Based on interviews with seven eyewitnesses, Doe (2003) concluded

♦ An examination of the original autographed manuscript by Doe (2005) reveals

♦ After living with the tribe for two years, Doe (2004) reported that

♦ In an experiment with a more rigorous research model, Doe (2001) has corrected

The length of your credibility-establishing introduction depends on three factors:

♦ **How much of the source you use.** The amount of space you devote to a source, whether by quotation, summary, or paraphrase, indicates to some extent the degree of importance you place on it. The more you use of a source, then, the more space you should take to establish the source's credibility.

♦ **The nature of the source material.** If the source is presenting an uncontroversial historical narrative or providing some background information, a less elaborate introduction will be needed than if the source is providing analysis, expert opinion, evaluation, or judgment. Conclusions consisting of expert

110

opinions or judgments require the presentation of credentials to give them weight and persuasive power.

♦ **How important the source is for your argument or discussion.** If you claim that the source provides substantial weight in favor of your position, you will need to establish credibility more thoroughly than if you bring in the source only as a minor support or as additional information.

As the examples above show, most credibility-building introductions should consist of just a few words. As a rule, even for sources with the most important impact in your paper, keep the maximum length of your introductory comments to less than ten words, and use such a length once or twice at most in a ten-page paper. Do not ramble on endlessly about how important or famous your source is.

Provide needed background or context

In addition (or perhaps as an alternative) to providing information about the author, some information that puts the source material in context may be desirable. Explanation, history, contrasting ideas, the setup of an experiment, or other information will often be useful for helping the reader understand the source.

> **Example 8.1.1**
> Historical background leads to quotation, APA style:
> Even a few years ago, individuals who prepared their own income taxes using tax software would have to wait until the "final version" of the software was released or make two trips to the computer store: one to get the preliminary version and a second to get the final version. With the advent of Web technology, however, that awkwardness has changed. As Doe (2009) wrote recently, "Users can now buy the software anytime, knowing that an up-to-the-minute update is available twenty-four hours a day on the company's Web site" (pp. 61-62).

Pronounced impact can be created by describing a problem or question that the source then solves, answers, or at least discusses.

> **Example 8.1.2**
> Problem statement leads to quotation, MLA style:
> William Shakespeare had barely breathed his last before the controversy began over the authorship of the plays and other works attributed to him. Over the years, more than fifty candidates (including Queen Elizabeth) have been named, either individually or in groups, as writers of the works. The controversy has not been trivial, either: Mountains of tantalizing evidence have been brought together for each of the top half-dozen candidates (including Shakespeare himself). Renaissance scholar Jane Doe argues that the issue is not likely to be resolved anytime soon: "Each of the principal candidates such as Bacon and de Vere has too much circumstantial evidence to ignore and yet not enough to be finally convincing" (654).

Recommend the source

In Chapter 4, you learned how helpful it can be to direct your reader's understanding of the role of a source by using appropriate introductory lead-ins, such as "Jane Doe agrees," or "Jane Doe has the opposite opinion." It can be equally useful and effective to recommend to the reader that particular attention to a source is desirable:

- ◆ Interestingly enough, John Doe reported that
- ◆ The most significant finding, however, comes from Jane Doe, who
- ◆ Doe identified an important detail:
- ◆ The most insightful connection, however, is made by John Doe
- ◆ Then, in 2006, Jane Doe developed a powerful synthesis
- ◆ Indeed, as Doe suggested,

In this last example, the word *indeed* is functioning as a sentential adverb, a word or phrase used to emphasize the importance of the coming statement. Use of a sentential adverb at the beginning of a sentence lets your reader know that what follows is especially significant. See the table below for other choices.

SENTENTIAL ADVERBS

assuredly	in brief	remarkably
certainly	indeed	significantly
clearly	in fact	specifically
definitely	in short	surprisingly
evidently	of course	to be sure
importantly	on the whole	without doubt

Caution: Take care to be moderate in your recommendation. Avoid unprofessional or overly enthusiastic language, such as *amazingly, incredibly, wonderfully, brilliantly, convincingly*, and the like. Similarly, you should avoid emphasizing the importance of more than just a few sources. Remember the proverb, "Where everything is important, nothing is important." So, to make the emphasis stand out, it's best to limit your use of these words to less than one of every ten quotations, paraphrases, or summaries.

8.2 Discuss or apply the source

During the process of researching, thinking, and drafting, writers form many connections in their minds between the various materials being used. As a result of such labor, a quotation inserted to support a point may have a seemingly obvious link or purpose in the writer's mind. However, the reader has access only to the written words on the page, not to the writer's thoughts. Sometimes, therefore, a reader is left wondering about the role of a quotation or other reference. An important task for you as a writer is to be sure that the connections between elements are clear.

The purpose of a source is not always self-evident

Sources (quotations, paraphrases, summaries, even brief references) do not explain themselves. Imagine your reader looking at the last source you inserted and asking one of these questions:

- ◆ What is this doing here?
- ◆ How does this reference apply to the point being discussed?

- ◆ How does this help advance the argument?
- ◆ What does this quotation mean?
- ◆ What should I especially notice in all these words?

As a thinking stimulus for yourself, imagine your reader reading over the quotation or paraphrase and saying, "Okay. I read that. I know what Doe says. So what?" Your task is to answer the "So what?" for your reader.

Explain the source

The first way to help your reader understand the meaning and purpose of a quotation or other source use is to choose a good lead-in, as was just discussed above, and in Chapter 4. A good lead-in helps to explain the source in advance by identifying its function in the paper—the lead-in positions the source in the logical context of the argument. For example, instead of writing, "Doe says," which tells the reader nothing about Doe's role in the discussion, you might use "Doe clarifies this," or "Doe offers a counter argument." Then, after the source speaks, go on to explain or demonstrate how your lead-in is correct.

Sources often need clarification, interpretation, commentary, or some other explanation. You may need to draw specific attention to the significant detail or the main point you want your reader to understand if your use of the source is several lines long. As a general rule, the more of a source you use, the longer your explanation should be. In fact, a good rule to follow is:

> **Your explanation should be longer than the source material.**

Some writers keep a loose scheme in their minds: The introductory lead-in should be from a fourth to half as long as the quotation, paraphrase, or summary; and the explanation following should be twice as long as the material being cited. Such a scheme may not fit every situation, but the general idea is interesting: The longer your source use, the more lead-in is desirable to build credibility or supply background, and the more explanation is needed to apply the source to the argument of the paper. The logic of this seems reasonable. The longer the use of the source, the more importance it takes on (why else are you using so much of it?), so there should be a lot to discuss. Imagine a nine- or ten-line quotation with a one-sentence application following it: Your reader might think, "What's going on here?"

Just as the role of a source can be positioned for the reader by using an effective lead-in, so your comments can be positioned by a lead-in, also. On the next page is a table of interpretive lead-ins that will allow you to orient your reader's attention as you begin to explain the significance of your source.

When you explain or interpret the source, do not restate or paraphrase it. If the quotation itself is unclear, you should probably paraphrase it *instead* of quoting it. If the quotation is clear, focus your commentary on applying it to your discussion. The point is to avoid saying the same thing the quotation says. Note in the following example how ineffective a redundant comment can be:

Example 8.2.1
Quotation with ineffective commentary, APA style:

113

In his analysis, Doe (2004) wrote, "This bill for subsidizing buggy whip manufacture is ill-advised. It should be voted down" (p. 1414). Here, Doe says he is against the bill to subsidize buggy whip manufacture.

A better practice is to add a clarifying interpretation, the "So what?" that will help your reader understand the quotation.

Example 8.2.2
Quotation with improved commentary, MLA style:
In his analysis, John Doe writes, "This bill for subsidizing buggy whip manufacture is ill-advised. It should be voted down" (1414). Doe realizes that subsidies for unneeded or marginal products represent a poor use of scarce public resources.

INTERPRETIVE LEAD-INS

What does it mean?
Here we see
From this, we can understand
This means, in effect, that
In other words,

What does it not mean?
This does not mean, of course, that
No one would suggest from this that
This should not be understood to say
It would be incorrect to interpret this as

What does it imply?
With this comment, Doe indicates
Doe appears to be implying here that
The implications of this fact are
The inference follows that
From this, we can conclude that

What does it not imply?
It does not follow from this that
Here, Doe does not appear to be implying
This fact still does not rule out
Yet it cannot be concluded that

Where does this lead?
As a result,
As a consequence,
This leads toward the conclusion that
This discovery greatly strengthens

How does this challenge or complicate?
Such a fact argues against the idea that
This, then, becomes a second hypothesis
Here, then, is still another complication
These findings appear to contradict the

Be reasonable about the effect of the source

Remember that an argument is built by offering multiple reasons and by appealing to evidence. No one piece will be overwhelming by itself even though it may be quite strong. Therefore, be careful not to attribute more convincing power to one source than it reasonably has. Rather than claim, for example, that a source *proves* a point or that it provides *overwhelming evidence*, you might say that it *lends weight* to the argument. Other reasonable claims include these:

- Doe's argument here presents a sturdy challenge to
- This seems to provide the best answer
- Clearly, this evidence cannot be ignored
- The fact that this experiment has been repeated with similar results gives us a degree of confidence in the conclusion that
- This is a credible argument that deserves serious consideration

The point of being modest is that making reasonable claims will increase your reader's confidence in your ability to evaluate and present evidence in a scholarly fashion.

Provide an example to clarify the source's point

When a source treats an issue in general or abstract terms, you can aid your reader's understanding by supplying a clarifying example as part of your commentary. A concrete example creates an image in the reader's mind, making the concept more easily grasped.

Example 8.2.3
Summarized source followed by paper writer's examples, APA style:
In his discussion of household electrical consumption, Doe (2007) argued that of the more than a dozen electrical motors in a typical home, the "occasional use" motors add significantly to the overall energy usage (pp. 246-252). Examples of occasional use motors would include bathroom vent fans, range hood fans, and garbage disposals because they are used only on occasion rather than continuously, as in the case of a refrigerator circulation fan.

Comment:
After the writer of the paper supplies several concrete examples, such as garbage disposals, the reader will have enough knowledge of the term *occasional use motor* to follow the subsequent discussion with understanding.

Example 8.2.4
Quoted source followed by paper writer's examples, MLA style:
A common style of literary criticism in the eighteenth century, writes John Doe, was to "point out the beauties and defects of a given work, with the idea that the critic would help build the public's taste as well as improve art itself" (321). Many issues of *The Tatler* and *The Spectator* periodical papers by Joseph Addison and Richard Steele exemplify this practice.

8.3 Blend in your sources

Using formal introductions over and over to set off quotations can create a rough or even disjointed feeling to your discussion and inhibit the smooth flow that a well-written paper ought to have. Alternatively, blending your sources into your writing can produce a particularly effective paper by allowing you to maintain the desired feeling of continuity while bringing in your desired variety of quotations. By moving quickly back and forth from source to discussion, you show that you understand and can work with the source's ideas easily and fluidly. Using a blended structure means that you do not need to interrupt the flow of your own words in order to present the source's words. Your own voice continues smoothly.

Work your sources into the discussion

Often, the centrally important core of information in a source can be found in just a phrase or portion of a sentence. In these cases, you can quote just that piece. If there are several such pieces, they can be assembled artfully into your discussion. When you construct sentences from a combination of your own words and those of the source, take care that the result is clear, smooth, and grammatical.

Example 8.3.1
Blended quotations, APA style:
During an investigation of the site, Doe (2004) found evidence of "early disturbances in most of the graves" (p. 233), with seven of them "plundered and virtually destroyed" (p. 254) by grave robbers. As a result of this activity, he concluded that the "entire site is largely compromised" (p. 221).

Example 8.3.2
Blended quotations, MLA style:
In her chapter on "The Power of Prepositions," Jane Doe notes that a small change in prepositions can produce "a dramatic alteration of the actual meaning" of a statement (453). For example, the expression "made *of* chicken" means that "the product is manufactured from chickens" (444), while the expression "made *with* chicken" may mean only that there was "one chicken among a thousand horses" (447).

Combine quoting with summarizing

If quoting represents a regular-speed presentation of a source, summarizing represents fast-forward. By combining these two modes of use, you can regulate the tempo of the borrowing, speeding up and slowing down as the importance of the material warrants.

Example 8.3.3
Combined use, APA style:
In his article on Web search tools, Doe (2007) discussed the search engines, such as Google, indexing billions of pages of content; specialty search engines for subjects, such as law, medicine, and education; and search tools for the deep or invisible Web, which he found "a rich and expansive realm of treasured content not often enough explored" by the average Web searcher (p. 365).

Example 8.3.4
Combined use, MLA style:
In his article on Web search tools, John Doe covers the search engines, such as Google, indexing billions of pages of content; specialty search engines for subjects, such as law, medicine, and education; and search tools for the deep or invisible Web, which he finds "a rich and expansive realm of treasured content not often enough explored" by the average Web searcher (365).

Use *one long, many short* for powerful persuasion

Especially in cases where you are building an argument, a successful strategy is to quote and discuss one source at some length to demonstrate its support, and then quote or refer to two or three other sources very briefly as additional examples of support. This practice offers the benefit of showing that several sources support your point, while saving you the time and space of detailing all of them.

Example 8.3.5
Long and short sources, APA style:
Advances in communication technology, argued Doe (2009), rather than enabling us to make better decisions, have deprived us of the ability to think. A hundred years ago, he said, a message required "three days by horseback or three months by ship" to go from one person to another, allowing for "substantial thinking time by both sender and receiver" between messages. Now, however, we are connected "instantly by fax, telephone,

and Internet video," all of which demand instant, unthinking replies (pp. 464-465). Jones (2006) concluded much the same thing about our "thoughtless response time" (p. 114), as did Smith (2007).

Comment:

You may recall from Chapter 2 that the credibility and reliability of information can be tested by seeking corroboration—the determination that the information is supported by more than one source. Specifically mentioned was triangulation, finding three sources that agree. Notice in the example just above that the writer has triangulated the sources for the reader: Three sources are cited that agree with each other. The corroboration has been accomplished briefly, yet it substantially strengthens the point the writer is making.

8.4 Avoid ineffective use

Bringing in a source in an awkward or ineffective way can backfire on the writer of a paper by confusing or detouring the argument. When you use a source, then, take care to make its presentation as strong as your own discussion in the paper.

Beware of long quotations

Two crucial goals of your writing should be to keep your reader both interested in your discussion and focused on the central idea you are advancing. Lengthy quotations, and especially several lengthy quotations, tend to subvert both of these goals. No hard-and-fast rule about quotations exists, of course, and you can find many examples of books with half-page or even longer quotations as evidence that you may do the same. However, there are some good reasons to use great caution before using a quotation longer than about six or seven lines:

- ◆ **Long quotations look like padding** to many instructors (as was mentioned in Chapter 4). If a long quotation is not discussed thoroughly, it might appear even more arbitrarily inserted.
- ◆ **Many readers skip long quotations.** No quotation can be effective if it is not read. Readers following the discussion closely may think that they will lose their train of thought if they read a ten- or twenty-line quotation, so they may skim or even skip it altogether.
- ◆ **Readers may lose focus** when they do read through a long quotation; the subject captures their attention and they begin to think about the source's interests and argument rather than the role the source is supposed to be playing in your paper.

It is not uncommon for a long quotation to make only a single point that could be summed up or delivered in a short quotation taken from the longer one. Either form of condensing would make better use of your paper's space and your reader's time.

Example 8.4.1

Source, letter from a government authority regarding an urban legend:
We have investigated these claims thoroughly, subjecting them to our usual rigorous procedures for determining whether or not there is a factual basis behind them, and have concluded that the claims have no basis in fact. They remain unsubstantiated rumors

spread persistently and yet without any discoverable merit. Parties wishing to contact the agency for further information are welcome to do so. —John Doe, 2010

Comment:
One way to use this source would be to quote it in its entirety. However, you could make the same point (less boringly and, in fact, more powerfully) as follows:

Example 8.4.2
Abbreviated use, APA style:
In a letter on the agency's Web site, Doe (2010), chief information officer, wrote that the agency had "investigated these claims thoroughly" and that they had "no basis in fact."

If you seriously believe that your argument can best benefit by the quotation of more than forty or fifty words, your best approach will probably be to break the quotation up. Quote a portion and then discuss or apply that part; then quote some more. By breaking the quotation into several pieces, you will not only better maintain your voice in the paper but also more clearly preserve the flow of the argument or discussion. You also show more clearly what parts of the source you are addressing in your comments.

Avoid overusing one source

Whether or not you must include a minimum number of sources in your paper, be careful not to use one source too much. Overuse of one source can take several forms:

- **Citing the same source several times in a row.** Using a source several times by following the same order of presentation as the source (such as pages 234, 255, 276, or worse, pages 234, 235, 237) creates the appearance that the source is merely being summarized and transferred into the paper without any further processing, analysis, integration into the overall argument, or interplay with other sources. A better practice is to collect all your sources and arrange them in the most useful order before you begin drafting.
- **Citing a source sequentially.** Even when other sources are placed between sequential uses of a single source, the effect is much the same as that just described: The writer appears to be copying without thinking rather than constructing a purposefully organized discussion.
- **Citing a source too many times.** Regardless of the order or location of multiple uses of a single source, relying on a single source more than just a few times usually implies inadequate research and thinking.

When you write a paper of any kind, even a book review, take command of the organization of ideas and the structure of the presentation. Put the concepts and your comments into the arrangement you believe to be the most effective. Readers expect reviewers to engage the material and present it in a clear way, and many instructors are wary of reviews that follow exactly the order of ideas in the book: They know all too well that some students type a bit, turn a few pages, type a bit more, turn a few more pages, and so on, the night before the paper is due.

Begin and end each paragraph with your own words

Usually, it is best to avoid beginning a paragraph with the use of a source (quotation, paraphrase, or summary) because that leaves no room to set up the topic of the paragraph and introduce the source. Similarly, unless a quotation is used for effect (such as a proverb or provocative statement), it is usually best to end the paragraph by applying the quotation and then concluding the paragraph with your own further discussion. The same policy holds true for summaries and paraphrases.

Be sure citations match the references

Experienced instructors know that this piece of obvious advice bears reinforcing. The purpose of an in-text citation (both APA and MLA) is to allow the reader to find the full bibliographic entry among the References (APA) or Works Cited (MLA) at the end of the paper. Simply put, if the citation says "Doe (2006)," there should be an entry in the bibliography under "Doe" as the first word of the entry. If an article or other source is anonymous and the citation uses a short title, such as "Tea Trade," there should be an entry under "Tea Trade" as the first words. This cross-referencing from in-text citation to bibliography is also why the entries in the bibliography are alphabetized: to permit easy location of the cited works.

To avoid creating the impression of being an unskilled writer, you should be sure that every citation has an exactly matching entry in the bibliography, which is carefully alphabetized. You will also thereby avoid being suspected of faking a citation. Citation faking is a serious act of academic dishonesty, often found in connection with plagiarism and often punished similarly. Take care to avoid any suspicion of this dishonest practice.

8.5 Working with sources that disagree or conflict

In Chapter 1, it was mentioned that the use of sources that conflict with your position can strengthen your research paper. For this reason, you will want to locate and include some of these sources in your work whenever possible. This section contains advice about how to make use of them.

Identify the source of disagreement

Whatever subject you research, you are likely to encounter conflicting claims about facts and events themselves or about the meaning of facts and events. In order for you to choose which claims to accept and which to counter with other arguments, you should first locate the source of the conflict. Here are some reasons why sources conflict:

- ◆ **One source is outdated.** New facts may have come to light, new technological discoveries may have been made, or a new understanding may have arisen. For example, the account of a historical event may be changed when an old manuscript is discovered, explaining how the event occurred. New discoveries in biochemistry change our views of mental illness and treatment. Technical discoveries in computers and digital cameras quickly render even recent information obsolete.

- ◆ **The sources begin with different assumptions.** Assumptions, often unstated by the writer, underlie much of what is presented. People differ about what constitutes good or acceptable evidence, and what can be assumed without examination. For example, a writer who assumes that printed newspapers will soon cease to exist as the Web takes over their role is likely to produce an argument about information access quite different from that of a writer who assumes that printed papers will always be available.

◆ **The sources are using different definitions.** When a term has no fixed or universal definition, scholars must create a working definition—called a stipulative definition—which serves a specific purpose. When these definitions vary widely from scholar to scholar, the arguments and conclusions of a study or interpretive article can also vary widely. For example, terms such as *mental illness*, *binge drinking*, and *toxic waste* are open to widely different definitions. Thus, if one study claims that there are a thousand toxic waste sites in the United States, while another claims that there are ten thousand or a hundred thousand, the different definitions used by each author may be the source of the disparity.

◆ **Interpretations differ.** This may be the most common reason for conflict in sources. Several people examine a set of facts and create different explanations for those facts. (Indeed, a recommended exercise in problem solving involves creating several explanations for the same set of data. The problem solver can then examine these rival hypotheses to determine which tells the most convincing story.) The meaning of facts is frequently uncertain or ambiguous, so that equally careful and unbiased investigators can quite rationally come to very different conclusions. It is important to remember this fact:

> **Honest people can differ.**

For example, imagine the investigation of a crime scene. All the evidence may be present to the investigators, yet there are, at least initially, several equally plausible explanations.

◆ **The source authors have different values.** Values shape the choices of all of us. Decision making is a product of the available alternatives, the criteria we want our choice to meet, and the values we hold about the worth of each criterion. Analysis and interpretation are in a sense acts of decision making, so they, too, are shaped by our values. A writer who argues that building a dam across a river is a good idea because it will supply electricity and a writer who argues that the dam is a bad idea because of its environmental impact are using the same facts to come to opposite conclusions because their values differ.

◆ **Personal bias is present.** There are many varieties of bias or ideological commitment in every arena of learning. A few people value political agendas over truth. Many have strong commitments to particular viewpoints. For example, a writer who believes that most large corporations are corrupt will write an analysis of a paper shortage with different conclusions from a writer who believes that most large corporations are honest. For some writers, the government is the problem, while for others, the government is the solution. Because bias is often exhibited by an unrepresentative selection of facts, together with a slanted interpretation, two conflicting positions may both appear to be based on evidence.

Of course, these causes are often found in combination. For example, a literary critic who believes that a novelist's personal biography is irrelevant to the meaning of the novel will probably differ from a critic who believes that the novelist's biography is relevant. The resulting articles (or books) would differ because of different assumptions, values, and interpretations.

One important task to perform before you separate your research materials into supporting and opposing sources is to remember this:

The opposing source might be right.

Give some serious thought to the arguments and evidence in the conflicting sources both before and while you write your first draft. Even if you do not ultimately change your position entirely, you might find yourself altering your views to some extent. In other words, avoid falling into *either-or* thinking where you view sources merely as friend or foe. Allow a careful consideration of each viewpoint before you choose your position.

Criticizing opposing sources

At the places in your research paper where it becomes useful to introduce an opposing or conflicting source, you should provide an effective but fair response to the source. The response will depend on the reason for the conflict. Here are some possible strategies for criticizing a source:

- **An error of fact.** Point out the deficiency in the facts presented by the conflicting source. There are three possibilities. (1) The facts are outdated and have been superseded by newer knowledge. (2) The facts are inaccurate (they may be partially right and partially wrong), confused, or otherwise incorrect. (3) Not all the facts have been taken into account and the source's argument involves incomplete evidence.

- **A weakness in interpretation.** Point out the reason for the difference in interpretation and show why your interpretation is stronger (or why the conflicting interpretation is weak). Reasons for differing interpretations are several. (1) The interpretations are based on different assumptions. (2) The interpretations derive from different values. (3) The source is biased (be careful and fair in showing how). (4) There is an honest difference in the meaning of the data or evidence.

- **Failure to include a significant argument or fact.** Conclusions based on incomplete evidence or evidence selected in a biased way are open to criticism by arguing that if the additional evidence had been included, the conclusion would likely have been different. You may have read arguments where respondents to an argument say, "But this fails to take into account the fact that—," or, "But this argument ignores the issue of—." One caution is relevant here, however: Take care that the omitted argument is truly significant or central to the issue.

- **A weak or unacceptable definition.** Occasionally, a writer will create a definition that is too inclusive, too exclusive, or in some other way not acceptable. One type of unacceptable definition commits the fallacy of *begging the question*: The definition is written so that it presents a conclusion or eliminates the consideration of an opposing argument. For example, "I define *mental processes* as those thoughts of which we are consciously aware. Therefore, by definition, there is no such thing as unconscious mental processes."

- **An error of reasoning.** Point out the error or fallacy. Possibilities include the following: (1) A conclusion commits the fallacy of *hasty generalization*: generalizing from too little evidence or evidence that is not representative. (2) Another fallacy of reasoning has been committed. See below for examples. (3) The assumptions behind the argument are incorrect or objectionable.
- **Faulty methodology.** Professionals often criticize studies on this basis. Point out flaws in the source of data, the failure of the data to be representative, a flaw in the design of the study, or an error made during the investigation.

Avoid criticizing a source unfairly

When you respond to the arguments that oppose your position in a paper, there are several logical fallacies you should be careful to avoid. Fallacies are errors of reasoning that divert the argument from its proper focus. These fallacies occur most often when writers attack conflicting sources:

- *Argumentum ad hominem* attacks the writer personally rather than arguing against the writer's ideas. For example, "No one but an ignorant fanatic would make such an objection." In that case, responding to the objection logically with good evidence should be easy, so why resort to name calling?
- **Genetic error** rejects an idea because of its origin. For example, "We dismiss that remedy for gout because it comes from folk medicine rather than modern science." The issue should not be where it came from but whether or not it works.
- **Appeal to prestige** uses a person's or organization's fame as a substitute for evidence or argument. For example, "These findings clearly disprove the objection because they came from a Presidential task force." A good reputation (such as scholarly prestige) adds to the credibility of an argument, but no amount of fame should ever be a substitute for an argument or evidence. To claim superiority for one view over another based on which side has the more famous advocates is sometimes metaphorically called a *beauty contest*.
- **Straw man** presents an opposing position or evidence in such an unfair or exaggerated way that it is easy to refute. For example, "Those who advocate raising the speed limit believe that the thousands of resulting traffic deaths are an acceptable cost for getting them to their hot tubs five minutes faster." Caricaturing or misrepresenting an opposing viewpoint is not merely unfair to the opponent; the act also diminishes your own credibility and hence the convincing power of your argument.
- **Emotive language** uses loaded words to appeal to the reader's feelings instead of to reason. For example, instead of presenting arguments or evidence to show why a proposal is weak, the writer might say, "This plan will take us back to the nineteenth century." Notice that we learn nothing from this statement about the deficiencies of the idea. Another use of emotive language is to employ single words or short phrases that carry negative or positive connotations, depending on the writer's attitude toward the idea. For example, "Some researchers are trapped by the fantasy that Theory Y explains motivation, while others have been liberated by Theory Z."

Review questions

To see how well you understand this chapter, attempt to answer each of the following questions without referring to the text. (Write down your answers to make checking easier.) Then check your answers with the text. If you missed something important, add it to your answer.

1. What is the purpose of introducing a source?

2. Why is it important to establish the credibility of a source you quote?

3. What is the function of an *interpretive lead-in*?

4. Explain the concept of finding multiple sources that agree as an indicator of source credibility.

5. What are some strategies for criticizing an opposing source?

Questions for thought and discussion

Use these questions for in-class or small-group discussion, or for stimulating your own thinking.

1. When you read a book or article that makes substantial use of sources, what are some of the things that help you decide how much credit you give to each source?

2. Which techniques in this chapter do you think will help improve the persuasiveness of your own writing with sources, and why?

3. What are some places you might find background information or context to help set up a quotation from a source?

4. In what ways are you responsible to your reader and to your source when you use a source in a research paper?

5. What are some reasons that sources might conflict?

6. What does it mean to say, "Honest people can differ"?

7. What are logical fallacies, and how are they unfair?

8. Have you ever found a source that you initially thought was wrong, only later to conclude that it was right? If so, explain how your thinking changed.

Name _____ Course _____

Chapter 8 Review: True-false quiz

Directions: In each case, determine whether the statement is true or false.

1. To avoid the fallacy of the appeal to prestige, you should not mention a source writer's personal title, job title, or organizational affiliation.
   ☐ True   ☐ False

2. The more of a source you use, the more robust your introductory information should be for that source.
   ☐ True   ☐ False

3. If two sources present differing conclusions about the same issue, one of them must be factually incorrect.
   ☐ True   ☐ False

4. Sources that oppose your central idea are best handled by ignoring them.
   ☐ True   ☐ False

5. If you quote or otherwise draw on a source at length, your explanation and application of the source's purpose and role in your argument should usually be proportionately lengthy.
   ☐ True   ☐ False

6. Your reader's confidence in your argument is likely to be increased if you make moderate rather than dramatic claims about the persuasiveness of a source.
   ☐ True   ☐ False

7. Quoting and summarizing should *not* be combined because the result will be plagiarism.
   ☐ True   ☐ False

8. Using several sources that agree with each other should be avoided in order to prevent redundancy. Use no more than two sources that make the same point.
   ☐ True   ☐ False

9. Lengthy quotations sometimes cause readers to lose their focus on the central idea of the paper.
   ☐ True   ☐ False

10. In the same way you add a lead-in to a quotation or other source use, you can add a lead-in to the discussion or interpretation of the source.
    ☐ True   ☐ False

Name _____   Course _____

Chapter 8 Review: Effectiveness

Directions: For each paragraph below, comment on what makes the passage ineffective and say how it can be improved. (Note: This exercise uses APA citation style. If you use MLA style, convert the citations appropriately.)

1. The telecommunications industry is in turmoil. "The Internet is threatening to make long-distance phone calling free, for example" (Doe, 2007, p. 144). Also, the world may soon go wireless.

2. In an article on natural hair care, Doe (2006) revealed that most commercial shampoos are very damaging to hair. This proves that natural hair cleansers are better for you than commercial shampoos.

3. Doe (2004) reported, "Clay soils need amendments to provide a loosening effect" (p. 234). Doe (2004) added, "Water does not penetrate clay soils well" (p. 235). Another thing Doe said is, "Sand, therefore, can serve as a useful additive for soils of low permeability like clay" (2004, p. 237).

4. Doe (2004) reported that credible information about various Internet hoaxes is available by "consulting the FakeOut Home Page, which is operated by the AECH" (p. 144).

5. According to Smith (2008), warnings about the danger of traveling to certain named countries are occasionally issued by the United States federal government's Department of State, which decides "to issue travel warnings when the perceived danger of traveling to certain cities or countries warrants the issuance of an official position directed at the general public who might be traveling to the given country, perhaps on vacation" (p. 261). The warnings are issued only after extensive analysis of all available pertinent information. Smith continues: "The State Department recommends against travel to a country only when consideration of all relevant information that can be gleaned in relation to the situation, including place, time, and potential actions against a target points to a credible threat" (p. 267).

6. In spite of government reassurances, however, Doe (2009) provided a devastating counterargument, proving that there are no guarantees of safety with this product: "You could be killed if you use it" (p. 333).

7. Increased noise can be a byproduct of economizing. According to Doe (2009), "The refrigeration compressor became noisier as a result of increasing its speed by reducing the amount of internal windings in order to save manufacturing costs. Ventilation air noise increased as higher-speed fans (noisier in themselves) were used to push more air through smaller, and hence cheaper, ducts, which then rattled from the air velocity. Less expensive mounting techniques produced whole room vibrations, hums, and even thumps as equipment cycled on and off. We therefore experience today a whole symphony of noise created by the desire to cut costs" (pp. 234-235).

Name _____   Course _____

Chapter 8 Review: Logical fallacies

Directions: Identify the logical fallacy committed by each of the following statements.

1. This so-called argument is a bunch of junk—just a lot of empty babble without a bit of significance.
    a. *argumentum ad hominem*
    b. appeal to prestige
    c. straw man
    d. hasty generalization
    e. emotive language

2. The advocates of this plan would have us believe in an infinite stream of money, effectively buying one permanent solution after another without ever a single complication.
    a. *argumentum ad hominem*
    b. appeal to prestige
    c. straw man
    d. hasty generalization
    e. emotive language

3. This opinion comes from a medical doctor at the International Research Institute, so it must be true.
    a. *argumentum ad hominem*
    b. appeal to prestige
    c. straw man
    d. hasty generalization
    e. emotive language

4. Of course, with his mediocre education, Doe was unable to get a job at a first-tier university, and this fact shows us what to make of his theory.
    a. *argumentum ad hominem*
    b. appeal to prestige
    c. straw man
    d. hasty generalization
    e. emotive language

5. After interviews with sixteen subjects taking the economics course, we have concluded that lack of life experience prevents any college student from understanding interest rate fluctuations.
    a. *argumentum ad hominem*
    b. appeal to prestige
    c. straw man
    d. hasty generalization
    e. emotive language

9
Editing for Accuracy

Be sure to porfread.
  —Sign near a printer in an office

The last, often sorely neglected, step in writing a research paper is editing—the final cleanup where the typographical errors, misspellings, and grammatical mistakes are corrected. Awkward or unclear sentences are revised, examples added, and citations are checked. This chapter offers some quick reminders about proper usage to assist you in your final edit.

- ◆ Checking for errors in mechanics and spelling will ensure a neat, presentable paper.
- ◆ Clearing up any grammatical errors will help you maintain your authorial credibility.
- ◆ Remedying those common inelegancies of style will give your writing the professional feel it needs.

9.1 Why cleanup is crucial

It has been said that when airline passengers see stains on the aisle carpet of their jet, they conclude that the airline does a poor job of maintaining the aircraft *mechanically.* That is, they transfer the idea of poor cleaning to poor repair practices. Such a generalization is likely to be incorrect, but it can easily affect whether the passengers choose that airline in the future. The passengers cannot see the maintenance performed on the plane, but they can see the spots on the carpet.

The case is similar with writing. Readers cannot see the author or know firsthand about how carefully or conscientiously he or she works, so they take cues about the writer—how smart, how believable, how careful, how knowledgeable—from the writing itself, and particularly from the accuracy of the grammar, spelling, and mechanics. When readers see misspelled words or incorrect punctuation (the equivalent of the airliner's spots on the carpet), they conclude that the writer is a careless or sloppy researcher and thinker, too. In spite of the care taken to produce a thoroughly researched, closely reasoned paper, the content and the writer lose credibility. For this reason, *accuracy is crucial.*

Some students object that it's unfair to judge a paper based on a few misspelled words or mechanical errors. There are two responses to this. First, it might indeed be unfair, but it is the world we live in, where readers are too busy, unable, or unwilling to determine a writer's competence in spite of what seems to be evidence to the contrary, telling them that the writer just doesn't care enough to ensure accuracy. Second, it's not unfair after all, because a large part of meaning is conveyed through the expression—the verbal clothing—of the ideas. And that includes the issue of whether the verbal clothing has holes in the knees and stains on the pockets. In other words:

> **Form is content.**

After all, wuold your opinion of this book's acuracy and authroity be different if you noticed a few sepling and grammatical errors was present here and there?

9.2 Check your spelling

The most obvious indicator of accuracy is spelling. The simple fact is that readers do not trust writers who cannot spell. The most glaring of spelling errors is that of authors' names or the titles of works. Spelling these items correctly is simply a matter of copying. Writers who cannot copy accurately are often viewed as either careless, ignorant, or incompetent, and therefore unworthy of reading. If you wish your writing to be read with credibility, be extra careful about accurate spelling. Double-check the names, the bibliography, and the titles.

The other energetically waving red flag that puts readers off is the spelling of the same word in several different ways. Even readers who may forgive misspelling a word repeatedly (the same way each time) are likely to be put off completely if they see the same word in three or four different spellings.

Check for ordinary misspellings

Now that spelling checkers are a part of nearly every word processing program, spreadsheet, and e-mail client, there is little excuse for ordinary misspellings like *questioneer* or *alot*. If your word processor does not run the spell check as you type, be sure to run it before you print off or e-mail the final version to your instructor.

Check for autocorrect errors

Some word processing programs have an autocorrect feature that automatically substitutes the correctly spelled word for a commonly incorrectly spelled version. For example, type *recieved* into your word processor and watch the word convert automatically to *received*. This feature can be handy for helping you avoid common mistakes. However, try typing, *The Application Delivery Network (ADN) has several benefits*. If your word processor is like mine, it changed *ADN* to *AND*. When you are typing along, no doubt you don't necessarily notice these tiny subversions by your overly helpful software. During your final proofreading, then, watch consciously for autocorrect errors.

Check for confused words

Misspellings can occur by confusing one word with another similar word. These include words that sound alike, such as *to* and *too*, or almost alike, such as *then* and *than*. Because the substituted word is spelled correctly, the spelling checker in the word processor will not flag it. Therefore, it is essential to perform a careful "human eyeball" proofreading.

Use American spelling

There is sometimes a tendency among student writers to copy the conventions they see in a book or article they are using as a source. This practice appears to explain why many students use single quotation marks instead of double for quotations, and why they put commas outside the quotation marks—because the book they are quoting does. They don't realize that British conventions differ from American.

Similarly, quite a few words are spelled differently in British English from their forms in American English. A particular word processing spell checker using American rules may or may not flag a British spelling. For example, the checker in Microsoft Word 2003 flags *colour* but not *mediaeval*, and flags *banque* but not *centre*. It is up to you, then, to learn the most common spelling differences, and be consistent in using American versions.

Note: Of course, when you quote, you always quote exactly, following the spelling of the source.

Below is a brief list of example words with differences between American and British English spellings.

EXAMPLES OF AMERICAN AND BRITISH ENGLISH SPELLING DIFFERENCES

American	British	American	British
color	colour	analyze	analyse
labor	labour	realize	realise
neighborhood	neighbourhood	organization	organisation
liter	litre	defense	defence
center	centre	airplane	aeroplane
fiber	fibre	check	cheque

9.3 Watch your grammar

An excellent way to brush up your grammar skills is to look over a grammar review or composition book for ten or fifteen minutes a day until you cover all the areas about which you are still unclear. Many of these books contain sections that focus on the most common errors, and a look at those items might prove beneficial.

To give you a start, here are three of the most common grammar errors found in student writing.

Comma splice

A comma splice (sometimes called a comma fault) occurs when two complete sentences are connected to each other using only a comma.

> **Example 9.3.1**
> Comma splices:
> The leaves had a wax-like coating, the stems had thorns.
>
> The sandy area eroded rapidly, however, the rocky hill showed little change.
>
> A photograph of the footprint was presented as evidence, later, a plaster cast was introduced as well.
>
> The correlation between the two factors was not statistically significant, thus, there was probably not a cause-effect relationship.

As several of the examples above show, a comma splice often occurs when the writer mistakenly believes that an adverb (such as *later, thus, however, then*) can function as a conjunction to join the two sentences with a comma.

Comma splices can be corrected in any of several ways. Consider these examples:

Example 9.3.2
Comma splice corrected with a period:
The leaves had a wax-like coating. The stems had thorns.

Comma splice corrected with a semicolon:
The sandy area eroded rapidly; however, the rocky hill showed little change.

Comma splice corrected with a coordinating conjunction:
A photograph of the footprint was presented as evidence, and later, a plaster cast was introduced as well.

Comma splice corrected by subordinating one of the clauses:
Because the correlation between the two factors was not statistically significant, there was probably not a cause-effect relationship.

Note that trying to correct a comma splice by deleting the comma creates a fused sentence.

Fused sentence

A fused (or run-together) sentence occurs when two complete sentences are written without an indication of where one sentence ends and the other begins. Fused sentences occur less frequently in original drafts; more commonly, they are introduced during revision, where some writers remove commas they deem unnecessary or, as mentioned above, attempt to correct a comma splice by removing the comma.

Example 9.3.3
Fused sentences:
The paper fed from the tray the printer began to squeak.
The original telescopic star image is in black and white the computer adds the color.

Fused sentences can be corrected in all of the same ways used to correct comma splices.

Example 9.3.4
Fused sentence corrected by subordinating one of the clauses:
After the paper fed from the tray, the printer began to squeak.

Fused sentence corrected by adding a semicolon:
The original telescopic star image is in black and white; the computer adds the color.

Sentence fragment

A fragment is a piece of a sentence punctuated as if it were a whole sentence. Some writers use fragments intentionally for effect, but in many cases the fragments are unintentional and awkward. Often, the fragment belongs to the sentence next to it.

Example 9.3.5
Example of fragments that belong to adjacent sentences:
Minerals are added to improve taste. After the water is purified.

Most photo editing software provides saturation control. To improve color intensity.

Sentence fragments are corrected either by changing the fragment into a complete sentence or by attaching the fragment to the sentence to which it belongs.

Example 9.3.6
Fragment corrected by being changed into a sentence:
Minerals are added to improve taste. This step occurs only after the water is purified.

Fragment corrected by attaching it to the sentence to which it belongs:
Most photo editing software provides saturation control to improve color intensity.

Exercise 9.3: Grammar
In each case, identify the error as a comma splice, fused sentence, or fragment. Then rewrite the sentence, correcting the error.

1. Some early maps of the world were symbolic they were not used for navigation.

2. The cancer risk from this chemical is now in doubt. Although it remains controversial.

3. We should ask whether the sample was truly random, then we could better judge how much confidence to put in the results.

4. The lighting fixtures were delivered by truck yesterday, about 4:00 in the afternoon, we will install them tomorrow before the end of the day.

5. The boat's hull is made from fiberglass, with a foam core. Making it unsinkable.

9.4 Watch your pronouns

Pronouns are parts of speech that refer to nouns. Pronouns include *you, we, it, he, she,* and *they*. Incorrect use of pronouns is a common source of writing errors.

Pronoun agreement

When you use a pronoun, it must agree in number (singular or plural) with the noun to which it refers. A frequent error is to use a plural pronoun to refer to a singular noun. To produce a grammatical construction, the noun and the pronoun must be either both singular or both plural. Note the following errors and their corrections:

Example 9.4.1
Original with error:
The company announced higher earnings. They will be increasing their dividend.

131

Improved versions:
The company announced higher earnings. It will be increasing its dividend.
Company executives announced higher earnings. They will be increasing the dividend.

Example 9.4.2
Original with error:
We asked the committee for a delay, but they said no.

Improved versions:
We asked the committee for a delay, but it said no.
We asked the members of the committee for a delay, but they said no.

Pronoun reference

Another frequent error is the use of a pronoun without any noun to which it can refer. An isolated *it* or *they* makes writing unclear because your reader must guess about the thing or person you intend. Be careful, then, to supply a noun referent for each pronoun you use. And note that the unclear use of the pronoun *they* (when it does not refer to a specified noun) can often be remedied by eliminating the pronoun altogether:

Example 9.4.3
Original with error:
A study reported on how salty soil affected crop yield. They found varying effects.

Improved versions:
A study reported on how salty soil affected crop yield. Researchers found varying effects.
Researchers studied how salty soil affected crop yield. They found varying effects.

Indefinite pronouns

Indefinite pronouns refer to unspecified nouns. In the sentence, "Someone dropped this pen," the indefinite pronoun *someone* does not refer to a specific person. By comparison, in the sentence, "When Bill was here, he dropped his pen," the pronoun *he* refers specifically to Bill. Indefinite pronouns include *anyone, anybody, someone, somebody, everyone,* and *everybody.* All of these are singular and therefore, to avoid an agreement error, must be referred to by another singular pronoun. Note these errors and their corrections:

Example 9.4.4
Original with agreement error:
Everyone must make their own judgment about this.

Improved versions:
Everyone must make his or her own judgment about this.
Everyone must make a personal judgment about this.

Example 9.4.5
Original with agreement error:
If anyone misses the central point of the film, they can wait until the ending reveals it.

Improved versions:
Anyone missing the central point of the film can just wait until the ending reveals it.
The ending of the film reveals the central point to anyone who missed it earlier.

CHAPTER 9 ❖ EDITING FOR ACCURACY

Note: The singular noun *person* is often used in an indefinite way, also. Be careful to use a singular pronoun to agree with it.

The grammatical remedy of using "his or her" to agree with an indefinite pronoun is not very elegant, especially if used frequently. A better solution is to use fewer indefinite pronouns. Computer analysis of student and professional writing reveals that student writers use indefinite pronouns ten times more often than do professional writers. The result can be writing cluttered with "he or she" and "his or her." To use fewer indefinite pronouns, substitute plural nouns relevant to the context. In many cases, you can write the sentence without any pronouns. Note these examples:

Example 9.4.6
Acceptable but awkward:
When someone uses an industrial dishwasher, he or she must be careful not to be scalded.

Improved versions:
When using an industrial dishwasher, the operator must be careful not to be scalded.
Operators of industrial dishwashers must be careful not to be scalded.

Example 9.4.7
Acceptable but awkward:
A person should always take his or her coat to a night baseball game.

Improved versions:
Baseball fans should always take their coats to a night game.
Baseball fans should always take coats to a night game.

Example 9.4.8
Acceptable but awkward:
Everyone should write his or her name on the test booklet.

Improved versions:
Test takers should write their names on the test booklet.
The test-taker's name should be written on the test booklet.

INDEFINITE PRONOUNS: THE GOLDEN KEY IS *DON'T*

Indefinite pronouns can cause confusion, seem vague and even amateurish, and result in agreement errors. One simple way to improve your writing, then, is to avoid them unless you have a really good reason to use one. Instead, use a specific, vivid noun in place of the pronoun.

👎 Anyone who forgets his or her badge must sign in at the security desk.

👍 Employees who forget their badges must sign in at the security desk.

👎 Everyone should turn his or her computer on early so that he or she will be ready for the start of the Web conference.

👍 Web conference attendees should turn on their computers early so that they will be ready in time for the start.

133

Avoid the ambiguous *you*

A final problem with pronouns is the use of *you* to refer to no one in particular. It is common in informal conversation to use *you* instead of the awkward and stiff use of *one*, or even to replace *someone* or *people*, but that use is not acceptable in formal writing because of the vagueness and possible confusion that can result.

> **Example 9.4.9**
> Vague and confusing:
> When you pet your dog, you can see his tail wag.
> Everyone knows that when you ransack a house looking for illegal drugs, you often take the furniture apart.
>
> Not confusing, but still vague and now awkward and stiff:
> When an owner pets the dog, the dog wags its tail.
> Everyone knows that when a person ransacks a house looking for illegal drugs, the person often takes the furniture apart.
>
> Improved:
> Most dog owners know that when they pet their dog, the dog's tail wags.
> When narcotics officers ransack a house looking for illegal drugs, they often take the furniture apart.

Use *you* only to refer directly and specifically to your reader, not as a substitute for *someone*. Note also that while business writing continues to grow more informal and direct, often using *you* and *I*, most academic papers are intended to be written at a more formal level. Consult your instructor to learn the level of formality expected.

Exercise 9.4: Pronouns

Directions: Each of the following sentences contains an incorrect or ineffective use of a pronoun. Rewrite each sentence, correcting the error or improving the effectiveness.

1. The organization has not yet released a statement, but they should do so soon.

2. Some hoaxes are very believable. When you first hear them, you are deceived by the details, even though you realize later that the details cannot be checked.

3. A report was issued regarding the cause of the accident, in which they said it was weather related.

4. The theft of the Web site's database means that anyone who purchased an item from the site has had their credit card information stolen.

5. If you need more tax forms, visit your local post office. They have a good supply.

9.5 Check for common errors

Here are several common mistakes, sometimes made simply from haste or lack of attention. A careful proofreading usually cleans these up.

Possessives

Nouns that become adjectives of possession are formed by adding an apostrophe and *s* to the singular: *tonight's weather, this student's idea*. Possessive plurals add an apostrophe to the plural noun: *workers' hats, men's socks*.

Oddly, some possessive pronouns end in *s* but do not have apostrophes; they are considered possessive words in themselves: *its, his, theirs, hers*. Most often confused are *its* and *it's*. *Its* means "belonging to it," while *it's* is a contraction for *it is* or *it has*.

> **Example 9.5.1**
> The label on the vitamin bottle lists its ingredients. [ingredients belonging to it]
> It's been an exciting research project. [it has been]
> It's an interesting theory, with many provocative elements. [it is]

Subject-verb agreement

A subject-verb agreement error often occurs when an intervening phrase causes confusion about the true subject of the sentence. Especially problematic are prepositional phrases beginning with *of* placed between the subject and the verb. When the subject is singular and the object of the preposition is plural, an agreement error can occur.

> **Example 9.5.2**
> Subject-verb agreement errors because of intervening phrase:
> This collection of software applications are on sale.
> This green wire in the bundle of wires serve as the ground wire.
>
> Corrected versions:
> This collection of software applications is on sale.
> This green wire in the bundle of wires serves as the ground wire.

Dangling modifier

You will recall from grammar class that adjectives are usually placed right in front of the nouns they modify. For example, in the phrase *widescreen projector*, the adjective *widescreen* is directly in front of the noun it describes, *projector*. That's easy to keep straight. When the adjective is a long phrase, the same rule applies. In the sentence, *Drilling for oil in a previously unexplored area, the oil company took an enormous risk*, the adjective phrase *drilling for oil in a previously unexplored area* modifies the noun right after it, *oil company*.

A dangling modifier occurs when the noun following the adjective phrase is not the noun that the writer intended for the phrase to modify. Look at these examples.

> **Example 9.5.3**
> Dangling modifiers:
> Reading the novel at night, the headless zombies made me feel afraid.
> Using laser thermography to measure temperature changes in the hive, the bees could be studied in yet another aspect of their social collaboration.

If we are to believe these sentences as written, headless zombies can read novels, and bees use laser thermography—all because the wrong nouns follow the modifiers. To correct dangling modifiers, put the right noun in the right place:

> **Example 9.5.3 (continued)**
> Corrected sentences:
> Reading the novel at night, I felt afraid of the headless zombies.
> Using laser thermography to measure temperature changes in the hive, the researchers were able to study yet another aspect of the social collaboration of bees.

Remember that writing is not a game where you expect your reader to guess what you mean. Writing is a communication tool, a channel for conveying meaning from your mind to your readers' minds. The more invisible the channel, the more direct and effective the transfer of meaning.

Misplaced modifier

A misplaced modifier is an adjective or adverb placed where it modifies the wrong part of the sentence or where its modification is unclear. The most commonly misplaced modifier is the word *only*, which belongs right next to the word that it should modify. As a misplaced modifier, it is usually put too early in the sentence.

> **Example 9.5.4**
> Misplaced *only*:
> The research study only listed the data from the first six weeks of the experiment.
> The photographer only developed the negatives after he read the news account of the robbery.

In the examples above, the writer is telling us that the study "only listed the data," by which we conclude that the researchers did nothing else with it, such as analyze it; and the photographer "only developed" the negatives, leaving us to wonder why he didn't print them also. When *only* is placed in front of a verb, it emphasizes limited action. Note the difference when *only* is placed where it should be:

> **Example 9.5.4 (continued)**
> Corrected versions:
> The research study listed only the data from the first six weeks of the experiment.
> The photographer developed the negatives only after he read the news account of the robbery.

Affect and effect

Because these two words are common in academic writing, and because they are commonly confused, let's sort them out. The main source of error is that *affect* and *effect* share the same meaning related to influencing an outcome, but in these uses, *affect* is a verb while *effect* is a noun.

> **Example 9.5.5**
> How will a change in procedure affect the reliability of the data?
> What effect will a change in procedure have on the reliability of the data?

Exercise 9.5: Common errors check

Directions: Each of the following sentences contains at least one error. Rewrite each sentence, correcting the error(s).

1. Tape backup should only be run at midnight.

2. Trying to decide on a new approach to the novel, the dead spider in the barn suggested a possibility to Jan.

3. The case of organically grown, extra-large, smoky-flavored almonds were on the upper shelf.

4. Its been a long time since we discussed the disclaimer on the label, together with it's implications.

5. How will the runoff from the upper area effect the water quality of the bay?

9.6 Some hints about style

In addition to correcting typographical, grammatical, and spelling errors, your final cleanup should include a look at your sentences and paragraphs to be sure they are clear and well written.

Transitions of logic

Transitions of logic consist of words or phrases that convey "logical intent": that is, they show the logical connection between two ideas. Since there are several possible logical connections (such as time, purpose, contrast), there are several categories of transitions of logic. The table on the next page lists many of these transitions, arranged by category and listed as milder or stronger. (Note that there is some double listing because of the different ways words can be used.) The usual advice for incorporating logical transitions into your writing follows.

- ♦ Use transitions between paragraphs to signal connections (addition, contrast, and so forth) between idea segments. Use transitions within paragraphs to signal a change from one sentence to another or from one section of the paragraph to another.
- ♦ Use sufficient transitions to provide coherence (holding together, like glue) and continuity (making the thought process easy to follow).
- ♦ Avoid using too many strong transitions. Be careful to avoid littering your writing with *however* and *nevertheless*. Use strong transitions sparingly.
- ♦ Transitions become stronger when they are placed at the beginning (or end) of a sentence, milder (or less strong) when they are moved into the sentence. Generally, moving transitions into the sentence is the better choice.

Example 9.6.1
Stronger at beginning:
Another example of a succulent plant is the barrel cactus.

However, American gold jewelry is less pure than European.
Therefore, the argument is shown to be invalid.
Finally, the problem of contamination is an issue that must be addressed.

Milder moved inside:
The barrel cactus is another example of a succulent plant.
American gold jewelry, however, is less pure than European.
The argument is therefore shown to be invalid.
The problem of contamination is a final issue that must be addressed.

TRANSITIONS OF LOGIC

	Milder		Stronger	
Addition	a further x	next	additionally	first, second
	also	other	again	further
	and	together with	besides	furthermore
	and then	then	equally important	in addition
	another	too	finally, last	moreover
Comparison	another x like a	just as ... so too	comparable	likewise
	similar x		in the same way	similarly
Contrast	and yet	rather	alternatively	nonetheless
	but	still	at the same time	notwithstanding
	but another	though	conversely	on the contrary
	or	yet	even so	on the other hand
	otherwise		for all that	otherwise
			however	still
			in contrast	though this may
			instead	be
			nevertheless	
Time	after	now	at last	immediately
	afterward	recently	at length	meanwhile
	before	shortly	at that time	presently
	earlier	soon	currently	subsequently
	first, second, third	then	eventually	thereafter
	later	today	finally	
	next	tomorrow		
Purpose	because of this x	to do this	for that reason	to this end
			for this purpose	with this object
Place	beyond	nearby	adjacent to	in the front
	close to	there	at that point	on the other side
	here		in the back	opposite
Result	and so	then	accordingly	in consequence
	so		as a result	therefore
			consequently	thereupon
			hence	thus

Informality

Your instructor may have told you that research papers should be written in a formal style, which means writing on its best behavior. Writing is expected to be more accurate and more careful than everyday speech. For example, formal writing avoids colloquial expressions ("this idea is totally hot"), vagueness ("different people have different ideas"), abbreviated spelling ("tonite" and "thru"), and incorrect grammar ("everyone loses their rights"). Additionally, some common expressions should be avoided because they are unprofessional:

INFORMAL AND UNPROFESSIONAL EXPRESSIONS

Needs improvement	Improved	Comment
In this quotation, it says	Here, John Doe says	Use the writer's name.
The author is trying to say	The author [or Doe] says	*Try* implies possible failure.
In today's society,	Today	Avoid wordy expressions.
This proves	This shows [or indicates]	*Proves* is usually too strong.
This article talks about	John Doe discusses	Articles don't talk.
In this quote, he says	In this quotation, he says	*Quote* is a verb, not a noun.
This is a common ad	Advertisement	Avoid informal truncations.
We don't know the effects yet	We do not know the effects yet	Avoid contractions.
And this, I feel, is important	This is important	*Feel* feels irrational; think!
I may be wrong about this,	[delete the sentence]	Don't apologize for your ideas.

Review questions

To see how well you understand this chapter, attempt to answer each of the following questions without referring to the text. (Write down your answers to make checking easier.) Then check your answers with the text. If you missed something important, add it to your answer.

1. Why is careful proofreading and cleanup described as "crucial"?

2. Explain the meaning of the expression, "Form is content."

3. What is an autocorrect error? How can it be remedied?

4. Define a comma splice and give an example. Show at least two ways to correct it.

5. Define a fused sentence and give an example. Show at least two ways to correct it.

6. Explain the common pronoun agreement error with indefinite pronouns. Then give an example of the error and its correction.

Questions for thought and discussion

Use these questions for in-class or small-group discussion, or for stimulating your own thinking.

1. In conversation, do you bring in *only* too early? Are you able to correct this habit in your writing?

2. Now that you have read this chapter, will you be more confident about accuracy and proofreading than you were before? Why or why not?

3. Of the information presented in this chapter, what proportion did you already know? (Use a percent if you want.) Of the information you did not know, was any of it surprising? Explain.

4. The text mentions that "student writers use indefinite pronouns ten times more often than do professional writers." What are some strategies you can develop to reduce this ratio, so that you can avoid pronoun agreement errors and the "indefiniteness of indefinite pronouns"?

Name _____   Course _____

Chapter 9 Review: True-false quiz

Directions: In each case, determine whether the statement is true or false.

1. Errors in spelling and grammar can cause readers to lose confidence in a writer.
   ☐ True   ☐ False

2. The modern word processing spell check and autocorrect features eliminate the need for proofreading.
   ☐ True   ☐ False

3. A comma splice can be repaired by removing the offending comma.
   ☐ True   ☐ False

4. Transitions of logic take on a greater emphasis when they are placed at the beginning of a sentence.
   ☐ True   ☐ False

5. Using plenty of polysyllabic abstract words impresses readers with a writer's intelligence and credibility.
   ☐ True   ☐ False

6. The correct spelling of some words in American English differs from the correct spelling of those words in British English.
   ☐ True   ☐ False

7. Most singular nouns can become adjectives of possession by adding an apostrophe and *s*.
   ☐ True   ☐ False

8. In the sentence, "We only caught three fish last night," there is a misplaced modifier.
   ☐ True   ☐ False

9. In the sentence, "What affect will this have?" *affect* is correctly used.
   ☐ True   ☐ False

10. The sentence, "In this quote it talks about hospital costs," is acceptable in both formal and informal writing.
    ☐ True   ☐ False

Name _____   Course _____

Chapter 9 Review: Error check

Directions: For each sample below, identify any errors of spelling, mechanics, and grammar, and any stylistic shortfalls. Correct each error identified.

1. After recieving instructions from the judge about the parts of the law that effected the case, the jury room was opened and deliberation began. At first, the members of the jury was confused. They only talked quietly to the person next to him, but soon you could see their interacting animatedly with everyone in the room.

2. Here, Doe and Smith (2009) are trying to say that there research revealed a tendency for people to engage in inconsistent eating behavior when dieting. One person bought a six-pack of diet soda and a large bag of corn chips, another bought three diet-sized TV dinners, and eats them all at one time.

3. Its been many years since anyone could drive down the freeway without constantly using their brakes. The irony is, as Doe (2010) reveals, once lane capacity is reached, adding more cars to the road decreases the number of cars per hour the road can handle the traffic load has passed a tipping point.

4. I could be wrong about this, but I feel that John Doe has interpreted line 36 of the poem incorrectly. "The quiet rustle of distantly near leaves" can be analysed more easily by thinking of a real forest. Where someone is using a chain saw. In a real forest, the sound of a chain saw does indeed have a "distantly near" sound.

5. Electronic interactivity with learning materials is, of course, a major emphasis of modern instructional design theory, however, creating interactive print materials is also an affect of the emphasis on active learning. Merely adding visuals is not enough. You know how, when you get bored watching those PowerPoint presentations, you tune out the speaker? Participants need to participate.

References

Note: Virtually all of the example sources cited in this book are fictional, including those of John Doe, Jane Doe, Smith, Jones, and a few others. Fictional also are the Lighting Institute and the Tapwater Beverage Company.

The following list covers the actual sources referenced in the text, presented in APA style.

American Cancer Society. (2009, June 11). Placebo effect. Retrieved from http://www.cancer.org/docroot/ETO/content/ETO_5_3x_Placebo_Effect.asp

American Psychological Association. (2010). *Publication manual of the American Psychological Association* (6th ed.). Washington, DC: Author.

Harris, R. (2002). *Creative problem solving: A step-by-step approach.* Glendale, CA: Pyrczak Publishing.

Maheu, M., & Gordon, B. (2000). Counseling and therapy on the Internet. *Professional Psychology: Research and Practice, 31,* 484–489.

Modern Language Association. (2009). *MLA handbook for writers of research papers* (7th ed.). New York: Author.[1]

Reynolds, J. (1797/1965). *Discourses on art.* Indianapolis: Bobbs-Merrill.

VandenBos, G. R. (Ed.). (2007). *APA dictionary of psychology.* Washington, DC: American Psychological Association.

---

[1] MLA style:

Modern Language Association. *MLA Handbook for Writers of Research Papers.* 7th ed. New York: Modern Language Assn., 2009. Print.

Colophon
Body text is set in Book Antiqua 11 point.
Examples are set in Book Antiqua 10 point.
Headings are set in Eurostyle bold, 11, 14, and 24 point.

Book Antiqua is a typeface included in Microsoft Word.
It is a close imitation of Palatino,
a very popular typeface, known for its classic looks
and easy readability. The high x height
keeps the words readable at small point sizes
while the crisp yet formal design adds gravitas and sophistication
to the content it embodies.

Index

Notes